COURSE
COMPANION

OCR GCE ENGLISH LITERATURE

Official Publisher Partnership

Oxford University Press is a department of the University of Oxford.
It furthers the University's objective of excellence in research, scholarship,
and education by publishing worldwide in

Oxford New York

Auckland Cape Town Dar es Salaam Hong Kong Karachi
Kuala Lumpur Madrid Melbourne Mexico City Nairobi
New Delhi Shanghai Taipei Toronto

With offices in

Argentina Austria Brazil Chile Czech Republic France Greece
Guatemala Hungary Italy Japan South Korea Poland Portugal
Singapore Switzerland Thailand Turkey Ukraine Vietnam

Oxford is a registered trade mark of Oxford University Press
in the UK and in certain other countries

British Library Cataloguing in Publication Data

Data available

ISBN 978 019 8387596
10 9 8 7 6 5 4 3 2 1

Printed in Great Britain by Bell and Bain Ltd., Glasgow

Acknowledgements

We are grateful to the following for permission to reproduce and adapt extracts from their
copyright material:

Steven Croft and Helen Cross: *Exploring Literature*
(Oxford University Press © 2008) and *Literature, Criticism
and Style* (Oxford University Press © 2004)

Steven Croft and Robert Myers: *Exploring Language
and Literature* (Oxford University Press © 2008)

Richard Gill: *Oxford Student Texts: John Donne –
Selected Poems* (Oxford University Press © 2007)

Elizabeth Gurr: *Oxford Student Texts: Alexander
Pope – The Rape of the Lock* (Oxford University
Press © 2007)

Contents

Introduction

Important note: When using this introduction, you should remember that the OCR GCE specification for English Literature is the document on which assessment is based and the document that you should refer to first where you need to clarify any part of it. The specification gives you full information on the content and skills that you will need to cover during your course of study.

The new OCR GCE in English Literature is made up of four units, two at AS Level and two more at A2. This introduction will guide you through the specification for each one, and also introduce you to the Assessment Objectives that apply to each unit.

AS Unit F661: Poetry and Prose 1800–1945

Unit F661 is examined by a **written paper lasting two hours** and carries **60%** of the marks of the English Literature AS Level. The unit is worth a total of **60 marks** and it is a closed text examination, which means that you can not bring your copy of the poems or prose texts in with you.

The unit is split into two sections:

- Section A: Poetry 1800–1945
- Section B: Prose 1800–1945

Section A: Poetry

For this section, you will study a set selection of poems by one of four different poets. The poets are*:

- William Wordsworth (1770–1850)
- Christina Rossetti (1830–1894)
- Wilfred Owen (1893–1918)
- Robert Frost (1874–1963)

*The set poets and poems will change from June 2012, so make sure you check the specification for information after this date.

In the exam, you will answer **one** question on **one** poem by your chosen poet.

Section B: Prose

For this section of the exam, you will study one of six set novels, written between 1800 and 1945. The texts (with dates of first publication) are*:

- *Pride and Prejudice* by Jane Austen (1813)
- *Wuthering Heights* by Emily Brontë (1847)
- *Tess of the D'Urbervilles* by Thomas Hardy (1891)
- *The Age of Innocence* by Edith Wharton (1920)
- *The Great Gatsby* by F. Scott Fitzgerald (1925)
- *A Handful of Dust* by Evelyn Waugh (1934)

*The set texts will change from June 2012, so make sure you check the specification for information after this date.

There will be a **choice of two questions** on each set text, and you will answer **one** of these questions.

As part of the study of your chosen novel, you will also need to support your reading and understanding by considering the interpretations of other readers. These readers might be your teachers or fellow students, but you should also study at least one or more selections from critical texts. These might include the four literary critical texts suggested by OCR, but this is not compulsory. You do not need to read these as complete texts, you can read them as extracts and select relevant material from them, or from other similar texts.

Assessment Objectives

In this unit, the Examiner will mark your work on the basis of four Assessment Objectives: AO1, AO2, AO3 (for Section B only) and AO4.

AO1: Articulate <u>creative, informed</u> and <u>relevant</u> responses to literary texts, using <u>appropriate terminology and concepts</u>, and <u>coherent, accurate written expression</u>.

This means that:

- you should be able to respond imaginatively to the text in question
- you should have a good level of awareness of the writer, the genres of poetry and novel-writing, and of the work of other writers from the same period
- you should be familiar with terminology and concepts like irony, narrative voice, structure and meter
- you should write clearly, ensuring that your spelling, punctuation and grammar are of a high standard.

AO2: Demonstrate <u>detailed critical understanding</u> in <u>analysing</u> the ways in which <u>structure, form and language</u> shape meanings in literary texts.

This means that you will need to read the text closely and show how each writer creates effects through choices of language, form and structure. *This is the dominant (most important) Assessment Objective in Unit F661.*

AO3: Explore connections and comparisons between different literary texts, <u>informed by interpretations of other readers</u>.

This Assessment Objective applies to Section B of this unit and you only need to focus on the second half of it, which relates to the 'interpretations of other readers'. Your response to this objective may be supported by the critical reading that you have read alongside your chosen novel in Section B, but you may find information about different interpretations of your text from other sources. You do not need to quote from these sources, but you do need to show that your study of the set novel has been enhanced by the interpretations of other readers.

AO4: Demonstrate <u>understanding of the significance and influence of the contexts</u> in which literary texts are <u>written and received</u>.

For Section A, this Assessment Objective means that you will need to show how the set poem relates to the wider group of poems from which it is taken. For Section B you will need to show that you have researched and thought about the influences surrounding the novel, such as:

- the writer's life
- the society in which they wrote
- how this writing compares to other works written in the same period.

AS Unit F662: Literature post-1900

Unit F662 is a coursework unit and carries the remaining **40%** of the marks at English Literature AS Level. You must submit a coursework folder of a maximum of **3000 words**, which will be assessed out of a total of **40 marks**.

In order to complete the tasks for your coursework folder, you will need to study **three texts**. All of the texts must have been written after 1900, and one of them must have been first published or performed after 1990. At least two of them must be literary texts (poetry, prose or drama), but they can be from the same genre.

To complete your coursework folder for this unit, you will need to complete **two tasks**:

- Task 1: A piece of close reading OR a piece of re-creative writing with a supporting commentary (**15 marks**)
- Task 2: An essay on linked texts (**25 marks**)

When selecting the texts for Task 2, your teacher will choose those that allow you to make links and contrasts between them. The links might be thematic or stylistic, for example.

Task 1: Close reading

If you decide to take the close reading option for Task 1, this means you will need to write a close, critical analysis of your chosen text. You should select a small section of the text (up to three pages, or 40 lines of poetry) and include a copy of this passage in your coursework folder.

Task 1: Re-creative writing

If you decide to take the re-creative writing option, then you will start by selecting a passage from your chosen text or poem on which to base your re-creative writing. You will need to include a copy of your chosen passage or poem in your coursework folder.

As part of this task you will also need to write a commentary, explaining the links between the original passage and your own writing. This should also be included in your coursework folder.

Task 2: An essay on linked texts

For this task, you will compare and contrast two texts and write an essay exploring the connections between them. Your essay should also show how you have been informed by other readers' interpretations of the text. Some examples of these 'other readers' might be literary critics, film or television interpretations of the texts, or if you are studying drama you might like to consider different theatrical interpretations.

Assessment Objectives

The two tasks in this unit will assess you on two different sets of Assessment Objectives. For Task 1, your work will be marked on the basis of AO1 and AO2. For Task 2, your essay will be marked on the basis of AO1, AO3 and AO4. The four Assessment Objectives are of equal importance in your assessment.

AO1: Articulate <u>creative, informed</u> and <u>relevant</u> responses to literary texts, using <u>appropriate terminology and concepts</u>, and <u>coherent, accurate written expression</u>.

This means that:

- you should be able to respond imaginatively to the text/s in question
- you should show a good level of awareness of the writer, the genre, and of the work of other writers from the same period
- you should be familiar with terminology and concepts that relate to the genre
- you should write clearly, ensuring that your spelling, punctuation and grammar are of a high standard.

AO2: Demonstrate <u>detailed critical understanding</u> in <u>analysing</u> the ways in which <u>structure, form and language</u> shape meanings in literary texts.

For Task 1, this means that you will be required to read your chosen passage closely and show in your analysis, or in your commentary, how the writer creates effects through choices of language, form and structure.

AO3: Explore <u>connections and comparisons</u> between <u>different literary texts</u>, <u>informed by interpretations of other readers</u>.

This means that for Task 2 you will need to show how the texts relate to one another, and the ways that different readers interpret them. These 'readers' might be literary critics for example, or film or television interpretations of the texts.

AO4: Demonstrate <u>understanding of the significance and influence of the contexts</u> in which literary texts are <u>written and received</u>.

For Task 2, this means that you will need to show that you have researched and thought about the influences surrounding the two chosen texts, such as:

- the writer's life
- the society in which they wrote
- how this writing compares to other works written in the same period.

A2 Unit F663: Drama and Poetry pre-1800

Unit F663 is part of your A2 Level, and carries **30%** of your total marks at GCE. The exam will consist of a **written paper lasting two hours**, with a total of **60 marks**. It is a closed text exam, which means that you will not be able to take your texts in with you.

The unit is split into two sections:

- Section A: Shakespeare
- Section B: Drama and Poetry pre-1800

Section A: Shakespeare

For this section, you will study one of four set plays by Shakespeare. These are*:

- *Henry IV Part 1*
- *Twelfth Night*
- *Othello*
- *The Winter's Tale*

*The set plays for this specification will change from June 2013, so make sure you check the specification after this date.

In the exam, you will have a choice of **two** essay questions for each of the plays and you will need to answer **one** question on the play you have studied.

Section B: Drama and Poetry pre-1800

For this section of the exam, you will study **two** different texts from a set list. One of these must be a drama text and the other must be a poetry text. You have a free choice of how you might pair up these texts; the list of which is as follows*:

Drama

- *Doctor Faustus* by Christopher Marlowe (first published in 1604)
- *The Duchess of Malfi* by John Webster (first performed in 1614)
- *The School for Scandal* by Richard Brinsley Sheridan (first performed in 1777)
- *The Rover* by Aphra Behn (first performed in 1677)

Poetry

- *The Pardoner's Tale* by Geoffrey Chaucer (written in the fourteenth century)
- *Paradise Lost Book I* by John Milton (first published in 1667)
- *Selected Poems* by John Donne (written 1572–1631)
- *The Rape of the Lock* by Alexander Pope (first published in 1712)

*The set poetry and plays will change from June 2013. Make sure that you check the specification for information on the set texts after this date.

You will be required to write a comparative essay on the two texts. There will be six questions to choose from, each with a different focus. You can answer any **one** of the six questions, regardless of your choice of texts, but you will need to make sure that you discuss both of your texts in some detail in your essay.

Assessment Objectives

In this unit, the Examiner will mark your work on the basis of four Assessment Objectives: AO1, AO2, AO3 and AO4.

AO1: Articulate <u>creative, informed and relevant</u> responses to literary texts, using <u>appropriate terminology and concepts</u>, and <u>coherent, accurate written expression</u>.

This means that:

- you should be able to respond imaginatively to the texts in question
- you should have a good level of awareness of Shakespeare and the other two writers, the genres of poetry and drama, and of the work of other writers from the same period

- you should be familiar with relevant terminology and concepts
- you should write clearly, ensuring that your spelling, punctuation and grammar are of a high standard.

AO2: Demonstrate <u>detailed critical understanding</u> in <u>analysing</u> the ways in which <u>structure, form and language</u> shape meanings in literary texts.

This means that you will be required to read the texts closely and show how each writer achieves effects through choices of language, form and structure.

AO3: <u>Explore connections and comparisons</u> between <u>different literary texts, informed by interpretations of other readers.</u>

In Section A, this means that you should show how your reading of the play has been informed by the interpretations of others. These 'others' might include recognized critics or different theatrical interpretations of the play.

In Section B, this Assessment Objective refers to the way that you should look at the links between your two texts and the contrasts between them in your answer, offering a detailed comparison to show how the poet and playwright treat the theme or idea in the question you choose. Your response should also be informed by other readers' interpretations of the text, although this aspect of AO3 is of secondary importance in this section. *This is the dominant (most important) Assessment Objective in Unit F663.*

AO4: Demonstrate <u>understanding of the significance and influence</u> of the <u>contexts</u> in which literary texts are <u>written and received</u>.

This means that you will need to show that you have researched and thought about the influences surrounding the plays and poetry, such as:

- the writer's life
- the society in which they wrote
- how this writing compares to other works written in the same period.

You should also think about the genre in which your texts were written as part of the context.

A2 Unit F664: Texts in Time

Unit F664 is a coursework unit, and carries the remaining **20%** of your total GCE English Literature marks. This coursework unit requires you to write an **extended essay** with a maximum word limit of **3000 words**. The essay will be assessed out of a total of **40 marks**.

In order to do this, you will need to study **three texts**. One of these must be a prose text and one a poetry text, but the third can be from any genre. The texts may be from any period and they can also be taken from different periods.

When selecting the texts, your teacher will choose those that allow you to make links and contrasts between them. They might be linked by tradition or genre, for example, or the texts may be from the same literary movement.

Your essay should respond to a point of view, and will be a comparative study of these three texts, exploring connections and comparisons between them.

Assessment Objectives

You will be assessed on the basis of four Assessment Objectives for this unit: AO1, AO2, AO3 and AO4. AO3 and AO4 are weighted more heavily than AO1 and AO2.

AO1: Articulate <u>creative, informed</u> and <u>relevant</u> responses to literary texts, using <u>appropriate terminology and concepts</u>, and <u>coherent, accurate written expression</u>.

This means that:

- you should be able to respond imaginatively to the texts in question
- you should have a good level of awareness of the writers, the genres, and of the work of other writers from the same period
- you should be familiar with terminology and concepts relevant to the genres in question
- you should make appropriate use of the conventions of writing in literary studies, including references to quotations and sources
- you should write clearly, ensuring that your spelling, punctuation and grammar are of a high standard.

AO2: Demonstrate <u>detailed critical understanding</u> in <u>analysing</u> the ways in which <u>structure, form and language</u> shape meanings in literary texts.

This means that you will be required to read the texts closely and demonstrate an awareness of how each writer achieves his or her effects through choices of language, form and structure.

AO3: Explore <u>connections and comparisons</u> between <u>different literary texts</u>, <u>informed by interpretations of other readers</u>.

This means you will need to show how the texts relate to one another, and the ways in which different readers have interpreted them.

AO4: Demonstrate <u>understanding of the significance and influence of the contexts</u> in which literary texts are <u>written and received</u>.

For Task 2, this means that you will need to show that you have researched and thought about the influences surrounding the two texts that you have chosen, such as:

- the writer's life
- the society in which they wrote
- how this writing compares to other works written in the same period.

Your Course Companion

This book will help you to gain a number of the skills you will need to successfully tackle the specification. Chapter 1 deals with different types of literary text, and the ways in which writers achieve effects through language, form and structure. Chapter 2 looks at texts in context, which you will need to do as part of the requirements for Assessment Objective 4. Chapters 3–5 look at the coursework units, followed by revision tips and tricks and an Examiner's views in Chapters 6 and 7. You may also find the List of terms on page 90 useful as you progress with your studies.

You will find a CD-ROM at the back of this book, which contains a series of support materials that you can use alongside your course companion. The CD-ROM contains a range of activity sheets that will help you to plan your work and practice some of the skills covered in this book.

1 Studying texts

Objectives

- to gain an overview of different forms of literary text
- to develop and expand close reading skills
- to prepare for studying set texts
- to prepare to study prose, poetry and drama texts in relation to context
- to explore ways of writing about literary texts

Close reading

Skills in close reading are essential for AS and A2 Literature study. 'Close reading' means exactly what it says. It is the art of reading closely, paying great attention to details of language, in order to come to the best possible understanding of texts and of how writers create meaning.

For at least part of your AS or A2 course, you are likely to study a selection of texts which are linked to a particular context, time period or theme. You may write about these for coursework, but for the examination you will also need to be prepared to do what used to be called 'practical criticism' or 'critical commentary'. This can be a multi-faceted task. You may be asked to compare texts with each other or relate them to other texts you have read; you will also need to recognize features that make them typical – or not typical – of their time or period; but above all, you will need to demonstrate the skills of close reading.

Developing your skills

The best way to develop your ability to read closely is to practise, by reading and analysing as wide a variety of texts as you possibly can. The more familiar you can become with a broad range of literary texts, the more you will be able to recognize the features of different types of writing and to see the similarities and differences between them. The aim is to develop skills like the following, which you can apply to all aspects of your literature studies:

- to read and make sense of a text and recognize its most important features
- to apply your own literary understanding as well as ideas you have read about or been taught
- to know about 'how writers write', in terms of style and structure
- to organize your ideas in writing quickly.

Approaching texts

There are some methods of planning your approach which can help you feel more confident about close reading. Here is a suggested checklist of the things you need to consider as you read. As this list suggests, it is a good idea to begin with an overview or general point, such as the theme of the text or its overall effect, and then look at the details.

1 **Subject or theme:** What is the text about? (This may seem too obvious, but it is a good broad starting point.)

2 **Speaker:** Whose 'voice' do you hear in the text? Is it in the third-person or the first-person? If it is first-person writing, is it the voice of the author or is the writer taking on a role?

3 **Form and structure:** How does the text appear on the page? Are there any obvious ways in which it could be divided into sections? Usually we talk about *form* if we are looking at the technical aspects of how the text is constructed – its pattern of stanzas or paragraphs, or simply how it is set out on the page; the *structure* of the text relates to how it is constructed in terms of meaning. For example, it might break into two parts; one focusing on the past and the other on the present.

4 **Ideas and messages:** What is the writer *saying* in the text? The meaning may be different from the obvious subject matter. Look for ideas which may lie below the surface. Are there any signs of irony or satire?

5 **Tone and atmosphere:** Does the text have an overall effect on you as you read it? Does it generate an atmosphere or feeling, such as sadness, gloom, or joy? If so, what is it about the writing that creates this effect? How would you describe the writer's tone of voice?

6 **Imagery:** What kinds of visual images or 'word-pictures' does the text present? How does the writer use simile or metaphor? Comment both on individual examples and on patterns of images that you notice. Be careful to explain and analyse these examples in terms of their contribution to the overall meaning and effect of the text.

7 **Vocabulary:** What do you notice about the individual words and phrases which the writer has chosen? Do certain types of words recur? (For example, there may be several words relating to death, or fire, or childhood.) Are there words which seem unexpected or out of place? What effect do they create?

8 **Rhyme, rhythm, and sound effects:** If the text is a poem, does it use a rhyme scheme, and what is its effect? (Beware of simply describing a rhyme scheme without going on to say why you think the poet has chosen it and how far this aim is achieved.) Rhythm can be important in prose as well as in poetry. Are the lines or sentences flowing or short and jerky? Does the rhythm change at key points in the text? Other sound effects or aural images are created through the use of devices like alliteration. Remember to identify the *effect* of these.

9 **Conclusion:** Sum up how the effects and details of style that you have analysed come together to create a whole piece of writing. What has your interpretation of it contributed to your understanding of the subject that it deals with? Does it offer a way of looking at things which you had not considered before?

Please note that this is *not* intended as a formula to be applied rigidly in every situation. Not every text requires detailed analysis of each one of these points, but this checklist can act as a starting point and you can easily omit any aspects that are not relevant.

Comparing texts

This approach can also be used to compare two or more poems or short prose texts. You might consider texts individually at first, or create a table like the one supplied here to enable you to see the similarities and differences more clearly.

Comparison	Poem 1	Poem 2
subject		
who speaks/ situation		
form rhyme rhythm structure		
ideas and messages		
tone/ feeling/ atmosphere		
imagery similes/ metaphors sound effects		
vocabulary		

Examining writers' styles

In order to respond effectively to texts you need to think not only about what writers are saying – the content of their work – but also about *how* they write. This means examining the particular combination of literary devices, structures, and vocabulary which a writer uses and which go together to form that writer's individual 'style'. From your own reading you will know that some writers' work is easy to recognize immediately because they have a distinctive 'style'. However, it can be more difficult to explain exactly which characteristics make a writer's style recognizable.

As a student of A Level Literature, you will need to develop the ability to analyse and write about style. One shortcoming noted by examiners is that students fail to take account of this and do not engage in enough detailed analysis of how texts are written. It is easier to concentrate on the writer's use of language when studying poetry, but it can be tempting, when writing about novels or other longer prose works, to focus on the plot or the ideas and neglect to examine the features that make up the author's style.

Try thinking of style as the product of many choices the writer makes about the elements in the following diagram:

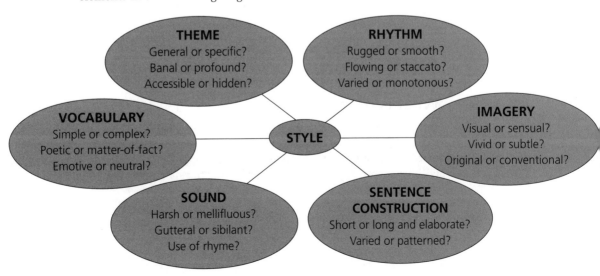

Thinking or feeling

Style can also be viewed as the expression of a writer's personality and preoccupations. The ways in which writers experience the world and the things which are most important to them are bound to affect how and what they write.

The psychologist Carl Jung puts forward the theory that people tend towards being **introverted** (more concerned with the 'inner' world of thought or imagination) or **extraverted** (more grounded in the external world of physical reality and other people). Stemming from this, he maintains that some people are *thinking* types, most at home with thoughts and ideas and perhaps less comfortable with the experience and expression of emotions, while others tend to be more *intuitive*. A third group are *feeling* types, relying on their feelings more than their thoughts to guide them through life. A final group are *sensation* types, experiencing the world via their physical senses.

This is a partial and simplistic explanation of Jung's ideas and many other people have created models to try to understand human personality types. However, factors like these are bound to influence the choices authors make when they write, in terms of content and style. They may also account for the fact that most of us respond or relate better to some writers than others. We naturally feel more at home with the work of a writer who experiences the world as we do, while reading the work of a writer who experiences it very differently may feel like struggling to understand a foreign culture.

Of course, most writing – the act of putting ideas and experiences into words – involves a rather cerebral or 'thinking' activity. Most writers craft their work carefully even if their aim is to use words to convey emotional or sensual experiences, but there are some who use more intuitive or free-writing techniques, allowing their words to flow without judging or altering them.

Exaggerating style

One interesting – and amusing – way of becoming more aware of a writer's style is to look at a pastiche or parody. The parodist usually takes the most obvious features of a writer's style and exaggerates them, as a cartoonist exaggerates physical features in visual images. A successful parody can make it obvious what a writer's stylistic habits are and help you to recognize them when you return to the original. Writing parody yourself encourages you to concentrate hard on the features which make a writer's style distinctive.

Studying prose

What is prose?

Literature students sometimes wonder what we mean by 'prose', expecting it to be something more specific than it is. In fact, prose is used to refer to almost anything that is not poetry, and so it includes a huge range of forms of writing. This section will focus on two particular forms of prose: the short story and the novel.

The novel

The word 'novel' usually means something new – a novelty. Some of the earliest novels, written in the seventeenth and eighteenth centuries, would have been just that. Jane Austen's view was that a novel was:

> ... only some work in which the greatest powers of the mind are displayed, in which the most thorough knowledge of human nature, the happiest delineation of its varieties, the liveliest effusions of wit and humour, are conveyed to the world in the best chosen language.

Nowadays we tend to make a distinction between 'literary' novels and popular fiction – but this dividing line can be blurred. As part of your A Level Literature course, you will be expected to study novels which are 'literary' and to develop the ability to recognize the differences. However, it can also be interesting to study popular, mass market novels and to consider how the conventions of writing fiction are applied in them.

The Victorian novelist Anthony Trollope once wrote that novels should be written because writers 'have a story to tell', not because they 'have to tell a story', but literary novelists have almost always intended to do something more. Early novels, like those of Samuel Richardson, tend to preach strong moral messages, although they can be rather sentimental; in the nineteenth century, Victorian novelists often used their work to expose social or political injustice, while novels of the present day may demonstrate the questioning of almost every previously accepted belief. All along, writers have set out not just to tell stories, but to convey messages or explore ideas.

Activity

In small groups, discuss some of the novels you have already read. Do you think they are 'literary' novels or not? How do you know? Create your own definition of a novel and compare your ideas with the whole group.

Studying the novel

Every AS or A Level Literature specification will require that you study at least one novel for the examination. This will probably be chosen from a list of texts recommended or set by the exam board. You may focus on the novel as an individual text, but you are also likely to study it in context, as part of a wider exploration of the literature of a particular period or theme. For coursework tasks, such as the extended essay, you may also have the opportunity to study and write about other novels you have chosen yourself.

At the outset, studying a novel can seem a daunting prospect. If you are asked to read a novel by Dickens, or George Eliot's *Middlemarch*, for example, it may well be the longest book you have ever read. If it is a twentieth-century novel which does not follow realistic conventions or a novel from an earlier period where the language is unfamiliar, you may feel that you will struggle to master it. Some novels are difficult but usually they are rewarding and a good read too, once you have become engaged with the plot and characters and you are more familiar with the author's language and ideas.

One concept we need to keep in mind when studying a novel is that there are two main attitudes or positions we can take. The first attitude is that what is important is the content or the world which the author has created. This is a world we can enter into, full of people, places, things, and events, to which we respond with liking or dislike, pity or criticism, as we do in the real world. Studying from this position, we will discuss the characters almost as if they were real beings with the ability to choose their actions.

The second position we can take is to see the novel as a 'text'; as a created work of art, and to look at it in a much more detached and analytical way. Characters are devices which the author uses and manipulates to create a particular effect. Their only existence is in the precise words on the page. Studying with this attitude, we will be more likely to consider what a character's role is in the construction of a plot, or the effect of using particular language to describe a place or person.

As you study a novel for A Level, you will most likely begin by responding from the first position, but you will also develop your understanding of the more analytical viewpoint. You will always need to know *how* the text is written as well as what it says.

Whether you are studying novels for the exam or for coursework, there are various aspects which you will need to know well. Questions or coursework tasks may be angled or worded in different ways, but you will be expected to demonstrate your knowledge of one or more of the following:

- **An overview:** You need to have a clear understanding of the plot and central ideas, how events follow on and are related, and how the novel is structured. Questions might ask you to show how the novel's structure affects the reader's response, particularly if it is not a straightforward chronological narrative.
- **Narrative viewpoint:** Who tells the story? Why has the writer chosen this viewpoint? How does this affect the reader's response?
- **Characters:** Questions often focus on one or more characters, their development or their relationships.
- **Setting:** The place, society or world in which the story takes place. Questions may centre on this, or may ask about the relationship between a character and the society in which he or she lives.
- **Language and style:** There may be distinctive qualities in the writer's choice of language, for example in the use of imagery or comic exaggeration. Questions will almost always expect you to consider why the writer has made these choices. What is their purpose and effect?
- **Context:** What is the historical or social background to the novel? In what ways is it typical or not typical of the time when it was written? Does it belong to a particular literary period?

Approaching the text

With a large text like a novel, you need to become familiar enough with it to find your way around easily. You need to be able to locate incidents and important passages quickly. Here are some strategies that will help you to gain this familiarity:

- If you have time, read through the novel fairly quickly before you begin to study it. This gives you the opportunity to gain an overall impression of the novel and to read it, as it was intended: for entertainment. You will see how the plot is constructed and develop an idea about what form of novel it is.

- Do some research. Find out what you can about the author and what was going on when the novel was written. If you are reading your novel as part of a study of a particular period, you will do this anyway, but even if you are not, knowing something about the historical and social background of a novel can help you to understand things which may otherwise seem difficult to grasp.

- Keep a separate log for your work on each text. Try dividing a notebook into sections. You will need pages for each of the main characters, the setting, the narrator, themes and ideas, and language and style. As you work through the novel, jot down your observations about each aspect in the appropriate places. Include important quotations and page references. When you need the information for a discussion or an essay, it will be easy to locate.

- You may find it helpful to annotate your copy of the text, marking important passages so that you can find them again easily. You will not be able to take copies of the texts into the examination but annotation can be a great help when you are revising. It is also useful if you are preparing for a coursework assignment.

Plot structure

Novels come in many shapes and sizes, from short novellas (more like long short stories) with a few characters and fairly simple plots, to large and complex works, with numerous characters, plots, and subplots and with many different strands which may or may not be interconnected.

There are also different genres or forms of novel. For example:

- **Fictional biography or autobiography** focuses on the life and development of one character.

- **Picaresque novels** follow a central character on a journey through life in which he or she encounters a series of adventures which form separate episodes.

- **Social or 'protest' novels** use the characters and the world they inhabit as a way of criticizing or protesting about social or political issues.

The plot, or storyline, of a novel can also be constructed in different ways. The simplest strategy is to relate events in straightforward chronological order, from the point of view of a single narrator. Jane Austen adopts this approach in her novel *Emma*, which was written at the beginning of the nineteenth century. However, there have been many variations on this. For example:

- In *Hard Times*, first published in 1854, Charles Dickens moves from one group of characters to another. The connections between them all are not completely clear until the end, when we realize he has constructed a network of threads which link them.

- Emily Brontë, in *Wuthering Heights*, another Victorian novel, uses two narrators and departs from chronological order by plunging us into the middle of a mysterious situation and then going back in time to explain how it has come about. She then repeats this process to show how the situation is resolved.

- In *The Handmaid's Tale,* written by Margaret Atwood and published in 1985, the narrative alternates between chapters which tell the story in the 'present' of the novel and others which are flashbacks. Entitled *Night* or *Nap*, these are times when the narrator has a chance to reminisce, dream or daydream about the past.

Narrative viewpoint

Authors may choose to write from a first-person or third-person perspective, or may even use a mixture of both. There are advantages and disadvantages in both and each offers different possibilities.

Writing in the first-person, the author takes on the role of a character (or characters) and tells the story 'from the inside'. This can strengthen the illusion that the novel is 'real', by making us, the readers, feel involved and able to empathize with the character. However, this usually also limits our perspective to this one character's perceptions: we only see other characters through his or her eyes. We cannot know of events the narrator does not witness unless they are reported by another character, for example in conversation. As we have only this narrator's words to go on, we need to ask how far we can trust the narrator. He or she might be biased, deluded, blind to the true significance of events, or even deliberately deceiving the reader. Often, this very question adds interest to a first-person narrative.

One particular form of first-person narrative is known as a **stream of consciousness**, a form in which the writer aims to give a sense of how a character's mind works by tracking his or her thoughts as they flow from one topic to another. When engaging with this kind of narrative, we have to piece together our impressions of each character from what the narrator reveals of his or her thoughts and feelings, actions, and attitudes to other characters.

Third-person narratives offer different possibilities. The author or narrator adopts a position which is 'godlike', or becomes a 'fly on the wall' reporting everything to us, the readers. This omniscient (all-knowing) narrator, from a vantage point outside the action, can relate events which may occur in different places, at different times, or even simultaneously. Often we are told how different characters feel so we see things from more than one perspective. Sometimes the author might tell the story dispassionately, without commenting or judging. Usually, however, authors make their presence felt. This might be through obvious authorial intrusion, where the writer butts into the narrative to express an opinion or comment on a situation, or it might be more subtle. For example, a character may be described in language we recognize as sarcastic, tongue-in-cheek, or ironic, making it clear that the author is critical or mocking; or positive or negative judgements may simply be revealed by the writer's choice of vocabulary.

The question of the writer's stance towards characters or situations can be quite complex. Even in third-person narratives, information is often filtered through the perceptions of one particular character. We may need to consider carefully whether the author's views match those of this character or not. Alternatively, the author may choose to write with a voice which is neither his or her own nor that of one of the characters in the novel. This voice may present another interesting topic for analysis.

> ### Activity
> Think carefully about the narrative viewpoint in the novel you are studying. Who is the narrator? Can you trust his or her narrative? How aware are you of the author's presence? Look for examples of authorial intrusion.

Characters

Much of the interest in a novel lies in the characters whose world we enter and in whose lives we share during the course of the story. We usually respond to them first as people. We can analyse their personalities, trace how they are affected by events and empathize or disapprove of them. However, we do need to remember that they do not have lives outside the pages of the novel and so it is rarely useful to speculate about their past or future experiences. More importantly, we need to pay attention to how they are presented.

Characters are revealed to us in various ways:

- **Description:** The author often provides an introductory pen-portrait and then builds up our knowledge with details as the narrative progresses. Key passages describe main characters or make us aware of how they change and develop.
- **Dialogue:** Other characters often give important clues when they discuss the character concerned. We may also find out a lot about someone from his or her own speech.
- **Thoughts and feelings:** The inner life of a character can be revealed directly, particularly in a first-person narrative.
- **Actions and reactions:** How characters behave in various situations will inform our view of them.
- **Imagery and symbols:** Characters may be described using simile and metaphor, or may be associated symbolically with, for example, a colour or an element. In Emily Brontë's *Wuthering Heights*, Heathcliff is frequently linked with fire and with the colour black. Similarly, in Thomas Hardy's *Tess of the D'Urbervilles*, Tess is associated with the colour red, which suggests danger or marks her out as a 'fallen woman' from the beginning.

> ### Activity
> 1 Choose a character from a novel you are studying. Then select three or four passages from different parts of the novel which show key moments for that character.
> 2 Analyse the passages carefully, paying close attention to how language and imagery are used to present the character at different times.
> 3 Using examples from these passages, write a short essay about the development of your chosen character.
> 4 Alternatively, choose an important character relationship from a novel you are working on and follow steps 1 to 3.

The setting

The imaginary world of a novel, into which the reader is invited, is often more than simply the place where the story happens. The physical environment may be important as a backdrop to the action but it can also be used to reflect the characters and their experiences. The world of a novel will also portray a society with its own culture, politics, and values. Characters may exist comfortably in their worlds, but often, the whole thrust of a novel depends on the central character being a misfit, or being in conflict with some aspect of their society, whether this is their family, their social class, a religious group, or a state.

The world of a novel can be as small as a household or as large as a nation. Jane Austen set herself tight limits, saying that 'three or four families in a country village is the very thing to work on.' *Emma* is set in Highbury, a 'large and populous village almost amounting to a town'. The action concerns only a few families in the village – those at the top of the social ladder, and one or two others of lower status, who provide material for comedy.

In *Hard Times*, the world Dickens creates is that of a northern English industrial town called Coketown: a larger world than Jane Austen's Highbury. Coketown is based on a real town, but has exaggerated features. Dickens uses this setting to highlight and to protest about the deadening effects of utilitarianism by presenting us with an environment where the physical surroundings reflect social conditions.

In Magaret Atwood's novel *The Handmaid's Tale,* the world is wider still. The novel is set in the future, in the Republic of Gilead, an imaginary state in America. Fearful about declining population due to man-made environmental disaster, a dictatorship has assigned strict roles to all people, but particularly to women. Wives are idealized, non-sexual beings. They wear virginal blue, while women capable of the all-important child-bearing are assigned to them as handmaids or breeders, dressed in red. Gilead is a state ruled by terror, in which it is highly dangerous to ask questions or to assert one's individuality in any way.

The setting of *The Handmaid's Tale* may also be considered to be an example of a 'dystopia'. A dystopia is a fictional world where living becomes a desolate or unpleasant experience due to excessive social restrictions or overwhelming problems in society. In Atwood's novel, these problems involve censorship, disease, oppressive state control and sexism. Examples of other dystopian societies can be found in novels such as, *The Time Machine* by H. G. Wells, *Brave New World* by Aldous Huxley and *Nineteen Eighty-Four* by George Orwell. Usually dystopias focus on problems in the real world, but these are exaggerated to the extent that they seem to dominate the lives of the characters that experience them.

In *Hard Times* and *The Handmaid's Tale*, the settings are very important. In both cases the writers have presented aspects they dislike about their own societies in an exaggerated form. This enables them to draw attention to these and to protest in an indirect way while being thought-provoking and entertaining. Whilst Dickens demonstrates the results of extreme utilitarianism, Margaret Atwood writes as a feminist, concerned about the environment and about women being defined and limited by their traditional roles. Both writers create worlds where people are reduced to particular functions. However, both have a hopeful note in that human spirit is not entirely crushed despite such repressive regimes.

Activity

Study and make notes on the setting of the novel you are working on.

1 What sort of world is it? How large or small, open or restrictive? What are its rules, values, beliefs, and customs?

2 Locate passages where the author describes the physical surroundings, comments on the social order, or where characters act or speak in a way which reflects their society.

3 Do the characters fit comfortably in their world or are they in opposition to it? Is this shown to be a good or bad thing?

Close reading

When close reading prose texts you will be examining literary techniques, such as imagery, choice of vocabulary, and rhythm. These devices will probably be more dilute in prose writings than you would expect to find in something like poetry but you will also need to think about the effects of different sentence lengths and structures, or the use of dialogue.

When incorporating close reading of prose into your writing you will often need to focus on extracts rather than complete texts. It is important therefore, to bear in mind the immediate context of the passage as you analyse it. Unless we are studying linguistics, we do not usually discuss a writer's use of language in isolation from its content. What we are concerned with is how effectively language is used to create worlds or present characters, situations, and ideas.

Some features of language to consider include:

- **Narrative voice:** The choice of first-person or third-person narrative; the tone of voice and how it is achieved.
- **Imagery:** The use of simile and metaphor. Look particularly for recurring images or patterns of imagery.
- **Sentence and paragraph structure:** The use of sentences which are long or short, complete or incomplete, complex or simple.
- **Vocabulary:** The selection of one word or group of words rather than another.

The short story

Many short stories focus on a single incident, moment in time, or experience, but that is not always the case. Not all short stories are deliberately crafted by the writer as a vehicle for a single effect. In fact some stories gain their impact because they do not follow this structure.

If you are studying a short story text there are a number of areas that you will need to consider. These are very similar to the aspects of the novel that we explored earlier.

- **Plot and structure:** You will need a clear understanding of what happens in the story, the basic ideas that it deals with, how it is structured, and how the various elements of it relate to one another. How the story is structured can be of particular interest if it varies from a straightforward chronological pattern.
- **Narrative viewpoint:** The question of who is telling the story is a very important one and raises questions about why the writer has chosen to present the story from this particular viewpoint and what effect this has on the reader's response.
- **Characters:** This is a favourite area for A Level questions. They often focus on one or more of the characters in the story or stories and may ask you to examine how the writer presents or develops the characters, or to explore how they relate to each other.
- **Language and style:** You will also need a clear idea about the distinctive qualities of the writer's style. This will involve focusing closely on the specific detail and the writer's choice of language (the way this is used, and the effects that it creates).
- **Connections and comparisons:** If you are studying a collection of short stories, you will also need to be aware of links between the stories, such as common themes and patterns, or contrasts between them.

Activity

Think carefully about a short story that you have read and make a list of the features that you think are important in terms of making this story 'work'.

Plot and structure

One thing you may have noted about short stories is that very often the story focuses on a single character in a single situation, rather than tracing a range of characters through a variety of situations and phases of development, as novels frequently do. Despite this however, the focus of short stories can often be a moment at which the central characters undergo some important experience which represents a significant milestone in their personal development. It can be seen as a 'moment of truth' in which something or some perception, large or small, changes within the character. In some stories though, this moment of truth is evident only to the reader and not the character.

Not all short stories reach a climax. Some stories may offer a kind of snapshot of a period of time or an experience – a 'day in the life of...' kind of story might be like this. Other stories end inconclusively leaving the reader with feelings of uncertainty, while other kinds of story do not seem to have a discernible plot at all. This may lead the reader to feel completely baffled by what he or she reads and to subsequently formulate a range of possible interpretations. This might, of course, be exactly the response that the writer intended.

This diagram presents one way of thinking about how alternative plots and structures of short stories work:

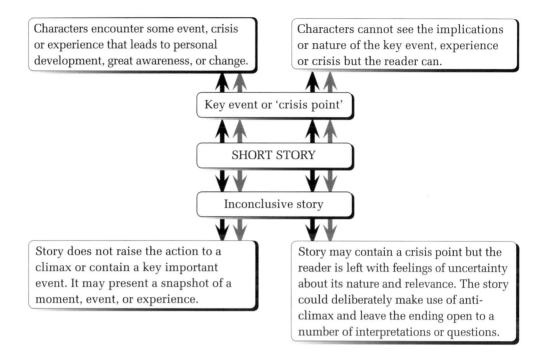

Beginnings

Our very earliest experiences of stories (the fairy tales we listen to as children, and then the range of stories that we read and see presented in film and television as adults), teach us one thing – stories have a 'beginning', a 'middle', and an 'end'. Strictly speaking, though, it is not entirely true. There are stories that do not seem to have a beginning or an ending in the conventional sense. The vast majority of stories, however, do have some kind of beginning or opening section; a middle, where the characters, situation, and ideas are developed; and an ending that draws the story to a conclusion.

Here are some possible ways in which stories can open:

- the writer launches straight into the narrative
- the writer sets the scene by giving explicit background information
- the writer informs the reader using suggestion or implication rather than direct description
- the opening is direct and holds the reader's attention, perhaps capturing attention with a word or short phrase.

Obviously the opening of a story is vital. If the reader's attention is not captured immediately, then the story contains no initial impact to encourage them to continue and to draw them into the story. However, bearing in mind the constraints of length under which the short story operates, it is also important that the opening compresses information, so that the reader quickly and effectively gains a picture of what is going on. Short story writers are often faced with this question of how much they can omit while at the same time creating the impression of completeness and continuity in their stories.

Narrative line

Short stories, like other fictional works, order the events that they describe in a particular way. Through the story-line the writer can create a wide range of effects, such as creating suspense, raising the action to a climax point, resolving problems, leading (or misleading) the reader in particular ways and leaving endings open to a variety of interpretations.

Very often the narrative structure is a straightforward progression with one event following another and moving towards a conclusion where all is resolved. However, sometimes a writer might play around with this structure to create particular effects.

Here are some points to consider when you focus on the narrative structure of a story:

- Make a list of the key events in the story.
- Look at the order in which these events are related by the writer.
- Look at the time structure of the story – is it told in simple chronological order or is there use of flashbacks or cutting back and forth?
- Are there any details or pieces of information that the writer omits, or particular points that are emphasized?

Short stories often have a moment in the plot upon which the whole structure of the story turns and which affects the outcome of the tale. Sometimes this trigger can be a quite trivial incident or experience but it signifies a moment of revelation to the central character. Margaret Drabble's short story, *Hassan's Tower* (Macmillan, 1966), contains just such a moment for newly married Kenneth on honeymoon with his wife, Chloë, in Morocco. Kenneth climbs to the top of Hassan's Tower with his wife and experiences a revelatory sensation as he looks at the people who have chosen to do the same. He feels as though, 'the details of their strangeness had dropped away, as though the terms of common humanity...had become facts before his eyes'. This moment of revelation is key to the structure of the story.

Endings

There are as many ways of ending a story. In a short story it is often the ending which reveals meaning, underlines a significant theme, or provides a resolution. This kind of ending should leave the reader contented and satisfied with a sense of a tale completed. Equally though, a writer might create an open ending, one that does not provide answers: an ending that might leave readers pondering on what it all means.

The ending with 'a sting in the tail' has become quite common in recent years, being popularized through the short stories of Roald Dahl. It is worth noting, though, that with this kind of ending we need to distinguish between a device which is merely used as a kind of trick, and a twist at the end which causes us to see something fundamental in the story as a whole.

Activity

Choose three short stories that you know and re-read them. Discuss the ending of each story with a partner, thinking about the following questions:

1 Does the story have what you would recognize as a definite ending?
2 How does the ending relate to the rest of the story?
3 Does the writer draw attention to any specific points in the ending?
4 How would you have ended the story?

Viewpoints

You are already familiar with the concept of narrative viewpoint. It is perhaps useful, however, to be reminded that this term can encompass two related but distinct ideas. When addressing viewpoint we need to consider the question of who is actually seeing the events described and who is narrating them. They may be one and the same or quite separate and the question is rather more complex than it might first appear.

It may be possible to approach the question of viewpoint by distinguishing between narrators who seem to address the reader directly from within the story (**internal narrators**) or those who have a more **external narrative viewpoint**. As a reader you need to be aware of how writers use viewpoint within their stories, be sensitive to subtle shifts and aware of the effects this can have on the narrative and your perception of it.

Characters

Earlier, we considered ways in which characters can be revealed to us in novels, and these methods also apply to the short story. There are, however, also some differences in the methods used in the short story. In a novel, the writer has many pages and chapters in which to present and develop characters in detail. Some novels have a timescale of years, in which we see characters grow and change. In a short story, which may only last a few pages and may only focus on a particular incident, or a few days in a character's life, the writer needs to give us enough information to understand the character quickly and economically. It is a bit like the difference in art between a detailed painted portrait and a quick pencil sketch. The sketch tells us what we need to know and our imagination provides the rest.

Although some critics argue that it is absurd to consider fictitious characters as if they were real people, when we read stories we do tend to create our own mental images of them based on our experiences of real life. However, we must not lose sight of the fact that they are creations of the writer and do not have an existence outside the text. In many cases writers create their characters to serve particular functions within the narrative and present them in ways that create specific impressions. Therefore, we should look carefully at the kinds of characters the writer portrays, how they are presented, which of their features are stressed, and what role they perform. We must also think about how the characters interlock with all the other elements of the story to create a unified whole.

Activity

Choose two stories that you have read and studied and write brief notes on how the writers reveal and present the central characters.

Studying poetry

Reading poetry

The study of poetry is a central element in all AS or A Level English Literature specifications: whether you are studying a poetry set text, looking at the poetry of a Shakespeare play, or writing on poetry for coursework. Even though the outcome of your work might be presented in different forms, the skills, techniques, and approaches that you need to use are essentially the same.

It is true that the poetry elements of AS and A Level English Literature present particular challenges. For a number of reasons, some poetry is only fully accessible to us today if we carry out a certain amount of research such as looking up difficult words, phrases, and references. However, responding to poetry cannot be taught (or learned, for that matter), in the same way that some subjects can. It is no good looking for some kind of 'secret formula' that you can apply to any poem.

Although most poetry is written to be read by others, and in that sense carries a 'public' voice, it can also be an intensely individual medium of communication and the responses it evokes can be equally intense and individual. Poetry often works in a very personal way and your response to a particular poem might not be the same as another person's. Words and images carry with them connotations that might trigger different responses in the minds of different people. So while it is often possible to say what a poem is about in general terms, the only really genuine response is that personal response that an individual reader feels.

This does not mean that anything goes, of course. For example, comments like 'I haven't a clue about this' or 'This means nothing to me' may be personal responses, but they are not much good in terms of creating a 'literary' response.

In this section we will look at some of the things that you can do to find your own way into a poem and thereby develop a more insightful and literary response to your text. Here are some general strategies for improving your understanding of poetry:

- Read as much as possible – become as familiar as you can with as wide a range of poetry as possible.
- Think about how language is used and make a note of any interesting features, lines or images that you come across in your reading of poetry.
- Think about the ideas contained in the poems you read.
- Read other people's responses to poetry – not as a substitute for forming your own views but as a broadening influence. (These responses can be found in various study guides, articles in literary journals, or reviews in newspapers or critical works.) They might suggest things that had not occurred to you or they might stimulate your own thoughts if you disagree with their view.
- Read poems aloud – either in company or alone. Very often reading a poem aloud helps deepen understanding and it certainly gives you a greater insight into features such as tone and rhythm.
- Adopt a questioning attitude. Whenever you read a poem, ask yourself questions about it. The three key questions to ask are: 'What is this poem about?'; 'How is it written?'; 'Why has the poet chosen to write the poem in this particular way?'
- If you are studying the work of an individual poet, reading beyond the set poems will help you to understand the particular poems you are working on.

Activity

Think of other strategies that you could use to help make your study of poetry more effective. Discuss your ideas with a partner and make a list of them.

Although there is no set formula that can be applied to poetry to produce the required response, there are certain features of poetry that you will need to be aware of in order to begin to appreciate how a poem 'works'; what the poet does to achieve the desired effect on the reader. Different critical books may refer to them in slightly contrasting terms, but basically these are the key elements that combine to create the overall effect of a poem. You may be familiar with some or all of these already.

Activity

Consider each of these aspects of poetry. Discuss your ideas in a small group and write notes explaining what each means.

Using these aspects of poetry to answer questions on the poems you study is a more detailed way of asking those three basic questions that we have already mentioned: 'What is this poem about?'; 'How is it written?'; 'Why has the poet chosen to write it in this particular way?' Answering these three questions will take you to the heart of almost any poem.

However, although we may look at elements such as content, form, and imagery in order to study their particular contributions to a poem, in reality they are completely interrelated and interdependent. The overall effect (and effectiveness) of a poem is dependent on all the individual elements within it working in unity (or acting in discord with one another if that produces the intended effect).

Content and poetic voice

In simple terms the **content** of a poem is what it is all about – the ideas, themes, and storyline that it contains. It is useful to begin a consideration of a poem by developing a general outline of what it is about. This is sometimes referred to as the **surface meaning** of the poem. Establishing this surface meaning will give you a framework on which to build the more detailed and complex ideas that form as your analysis of the poem develops. Sometimes it is possible to respond to a poem without fully understanding every word or phrase and sometimes meaning evolves as you continue to study a poem. However, having an initial idea or impression of what a poem is about can be an important first step towards a fuller and more assured understanding.

When considering the content of a poem it is also important to identify the **poetic voice** of the poem. In other words, decide who the 'speaker' of the poem is. In many cases the poetic voice may well be the poet's, but it may be that the words of the poem are spoken through a character that the poet has created or a narrator figure other than the poet. This happens in *The Canterbury Tales*, where usually a particular character is telling the tale. Geoffrey Chaucer (the writer) often then interrupts his character (his fictitious narrator) to address the reader.

Identifying the speaker also helps to determine a number of other aspects of the poem such as tone, mood, and the overall intention behind the poem. The poetic voice could be the poet's genuine voice expressing a heartfelt emotion or it could be the voice of a narrator expressing a view or feeling that the poet may or may not share.

Activity

1 Consider a poem that you are studying. How would you describe the poetic voice in the poem? Make a list of observations.

2 Join a group of two or three students and discuss your thoughts. Add to your notes in light of your discussion.

Tone and mood

The effect that a poem has on the reader is very closely determined by the tone and mood that it creates. As we have already discussed, a poem contains a voice and like any voice it can project a certain **tone** that gives the listener (or reader) certain messages. Obviously there are many different kinds of tone. The tone might be angry or reflective, melancholy or joyful, bitter or ironic. Just as the tone of voice in which someone speaks tells us a great deal about the way they feel, so the tone of the 'poetic voice' tells us a great deal about how the poet or the narrator of the poem feels.

The **mood**, on the other hand, although very closely connected with the tone, is not quite the same thing. When we refer to the mood of a poem we are really talking about the **atmosphere** that the poem creates. Very often tone and mood in a poem are closely linked and a certain tone produces a certain mood. For example, if the poet uses a melancholy tone it is unlikely that the mood of the poem will be bright and lively. Sometimes, though, the poet may quite deliberately use a tone that does not match the mood the poem creates in order to achieve a particular effect – underlining a certain irony, for example. The overall impact of a poem stems not only from the literal meaning of the words but from the tone and mood that they create. One of the most effective ways of recognizing the tone of a poem is to hear it read aloud.

Try reading poems out loud for yourself, experimenting with different ways of reading each particular poem. The more practice you get at this the better able you will be to 'hear' poems in your mind when you read them to yourself. The tone of a poem can be communicated to the reader or listener in many ways and it is through being sensitive to the poet's tone that we can begin to understand the intention that lies behind the words.

Here are some ideas of how tone and mood can be created:

- through the loudness or softness of the voice speaking the poem
- through the rhythm that is created
- through the poet's choice of words
- through the emphasis placed on particular words or phrases
- through the breaks and pauses that the poet places in the poem (often the things which go unsaid can tell you a great deal).

Imagery

Essentially the true 'meaning' of a poem lies in the total effect that it has upon the reader. Very often that effect will stimulate a response which is not just a reaction to what the poet has to say, but which draws on the reader's own intellectual and emotional experience. Imagery can be of central importance in creating this response within the reader.

The concept of imagery is a very simple one and although it is used a good deal in poetic writing it is, of course, found in other kinds of writing too. An **image** is language used to help us to see, hear, feel, think about or understand more vividly what is being said or the impression that the writer wishes to convey.

Images can work in several ways in the mind of the reader. On a simple level, an image can be used literally to describe something. Often, though, images are **non-literal** or **figurative**: the thing being described is compared to something else with which it has elements in common to make the description clearer to the reader. You will, no doubt, already be familiar with images, such as similes and metaphors, which work in this way. However, just in case you need it, here is a reminder of the difference between the two, along with a definition of personification:

The simile

Similes are easy to spot because they make the comparison quite clear, often by using the words 'as' or 'like'.

The metaphor

In some ways a metaphor is like a simile in that it too creates a comparison. However, it is less direct than the simile in that it does not use 'as' or 'like' to create the comparison. Often the metaphor describes the subject as *being* the thing to which it is compared.

Personification

Personification occurs when poets attribute human qualities or actions to an inanimate object or abstract idea.

Aural imagery

Some kinds of images rely not upon the pictures that they create in the mind of the reader, but on the effect that they have on the ear, or a combination of both:

- **Alliteration** involves the repetition of the same consonant sound, usually at the beginning of each word, over several words together.
- **Assonance** involves the repetition of a vowel sound to achieve a particular kind of effect.
- **Onomatopoeia** refers to words that by their sound reflect their meaning. On a simple level words like 'bang' or 'crash' actually sound like the noises they describe.

The important thing, however, is not so much to be able to spot the different kinds of images that might be present in a poem, but to understand why the poet has used a particular image and how it may work in the mind of the reader. Being able to say 'the poet uses alliteration in stanza three' is of no value in terms of the critical appreciation of a poem, but being able to show what the alliteration contributes to the overall effect of the poem is valuable.

For more on these individual forms of imagery see the **List of terms** at the back of this book.

Rhyme

Rhyme can make an important contribution to the musical quality of a poem, and like rhythm it affects the sound and the overall impact of the piece. The system of rhyme within a poem—the **rhyme scheme**—can influence this effect in a variety of ways. It might act as a unifying influence and draw a poem together, or it could add emphasis to particular elements of the vocabulary (or diction). There are various kinds of rhymes and rhyme schemes and although most work on the basis of the rhyme occurring at the end of a line, some occur within the line. These are called **internal rhymes**.

In the same way that rhythm in a poem often follows a recognized pattern, so does rhyme. Working out the rhyme scheme is quite straightforward and is done by indicating lines that rhyme together through marking them with the same letter of the alphabet.

Some rhyme schemes and rhyme patterns are described using specific terms. Pairs of lines that rhyme are called **couplets** or **rhyming couplets**. Sometimes a whole poem can consist entirely of rhyming couplets or the couplet can be used as part of a larger rhyme scheme. A Shakespearean sonnet uses the couplet to draw the poem to an end, as in Shakespeare's *Sonnet XVIII*, for example:

> So long as men can breathe or eyes can see,
> So long lives this, and this gives life to thee.

Rhyming couplets tend to create a bold, assertive effect and strongly convey a point or message. They can also be used for comic effect, to deflate an argument or character.

The **quatrain** is a set of four rhyming lines. Usual rhyme schemes are *abab, abcb, aaaa,* or *abba*. In *Jerusalem*, William Blake uses the *abcb* scheme:

> And did those feet in ancient time
> Walk upon England's mountains green?
> And was the holy Lamb of God
> On England's pleasant pastures seen?

The quatrain is a flexible form that is used to create many effects but often, as here, it produces a sense of unity within compact and regular stanzas.

A **sestet** is a six-line stanza that can be arranged in a number of ways. The last six lines of an Italian sonnet are also called the sestet. In '*The lowest trees have tops, the ant her gall*', Edward Dyer uses a regular *ababcc* rhyme scheme:

> The lowest trees have tops, the ant her gall,
> The fly her spleen, the little spark his heat;
> The slender hairs cast shadows, though but small,
> And bees have stings, although they be not great;
> Seas have their source, and so have shallow springs:
> And love is love, in beggars and in kings.

The **octave** is an eight-line stanza and can be constructed in a number of ways. It can be formed by linking two quatrains together or it can have a rhyme scheme that integrates all eight lines. It is also the name given to the first eight lines of an Italian sonnet.

As with all the elements of a poem, the important thing is not to be able to spot the use of rhymes, or even to work out the rhyme scheme, but to ask yourself: 'Why has the poet used rhyme in this way and what does it contribute, together with all the other features, to the overall impact of the poem?'. The answer to this question is what really matters.

Effects of rhyme

Here are some effects that rhyme might have on a poem:

- it can make a poem sound pleasing to the ear and perhaps add a musical quality; conversely, it can create a jarring effect
- it could serve to emphasize certain words – very often the words that rhyme are given a certain prominence
- it can act as a kind of unifying influence on the poem, drawing lines and stanzas together through the pattern it imposes on them
- it can give a poem an incantatory or ritualistic feel
- it can influence the rhythm of the verse
- it can give a sense of finality – the rhyming couplet is often used to give a sense of completeness
- it can exert a subconscious effect on the reader, drawing together certain words or images, affecting the sound, or adding emphasis in some way

Rhythm

Although it is by no means true of all poems, one of the basic differences between a poem and a piece of prose is that a poem can contain some form of regular beat, or rhythm.

Often this sense of rhythm can exert a profound influence on the overall effect of the poem giving it its feeling of movement and life. The poet can use rhythm to create many different effects or to emphasize a certain aspect or idea in the poem. Very often it is also an important contributing factor to the mood or atmosphere and to what is sometimes referred to as the 'musical quality' of a poem. Music can be gentle and flowing, harsh or discordant, stilted and uneven in phrasing, or regular in tempo. It can have a rhythm that reflects a serious or solemn mood or a rhythm that suggests the comic or absurd. The same is true about the rhythms of poetry.

Here are some examples of the ways in which poets use language to create varying rhythms:

Syllable stress: The English language possesses natural rhythms which we use automatically every time we pronounce words. For example, if we think of a word like 'delicately', it comes quite naturally to us to stress the first syllable and not the second. Not to do so would be to mispronounce the word. Poets often use these natural rhythms within words to help contribute to the overall rhythmic effect.

Emphatic stress: Poets sometimes choose to place emphasis on a particular word or phrase in order to achieve a particular result. The stress might be shifted to reinforce a particular tone or sometimes to affect the meaning. For example, think about Wordsworth's famous line 'I wandered lonely as a cloud' and how different emphasis can change the overall effect:

I wandered lonely as a cloud	I *wandered* lonely as a cloud
I wandered *lonely* as a cloud	I wandered lonely as a *cloud*

The natural rhythm of a phrase will often tell you what is right for the poem.

Phrasing and punctuation: The rhythm of a poem (or any other piece of writing) can be influenced by factors such as word order and length of phrases or sentences, and these in turn can be influenced by the choice of punctuation marks, line and stanza breaks, and use of repetition.

Metre: Technically speaking, the whole notion of rhythm in poetry is closely tied up with the idea of metre. This concept originated from the principles of classical Greek and Latin verse and was adopted by English poets from early times. Such principles stated that a line of verse should follow a precise and regular pattern in terms of the number of syllables it contained and the stress pattern that it used. This pattern was then repeated throughout the poem. Regular patterns of these stressed and unstressed syllables are called **metres**.

Metrical variation

Twentieth-century poets have tended to move away from strict metrical forms, but metre can still be an important element in modern poetry. By its nature though, metre is a mechanical and repetitive device which often is at variance with the natural rhythms that a poem may contain. Few poets stick religiously to the metrical pattern that they adopt and poetry should always be read according to the natural rhythms of the language rather than its metrical plan.

Remember when you are writing about a poem that identifying its metrical pattern is of little value in itself. You will gain little reward in an exam for simply mentioning the metre of a poem. The key thing is to explain what it contributes to the effect of the poem overall. Don't worry if you can't remember the technical terms – the main thing is that you are able to describe what is happening. Technical terms are a kind of shorthand way of doing this, but they are by no means essential. What matters is your understanding of how the poem works as a piece of writing.

Form

There are many different ways in which poems can be structured. One thing is certain though: a poet does not simply choose a certain form at random. It will have been carefully chosen and will have a direct bearing on what the poet hopes to achieve through the poem. In considering the form of a particular poem, we are back to that central question – why? In this case: 'Why has the poet chosen to use this particular form?'.

Form can refer to the way that the poem is actually written down on the page or to the way that the lines are organized, grouped, or structured. (This is sometimes called **poetic form**.) In terms of its structure, poetry can be divided into two categories. First, there is the kind of poetry where the lines follow on one from another continuously without breaks, such as in Wordsworth's *The Prelude*, Milton's *Paradise Lost* or Keats's *Endymion*. The technical term for this is **stichic poetry**, but don't worry too much about the technical terms; the important thing is to be able to recognize that poems differ in the way they are put together.

Secondly, there is the kind of poetry where the lines are arranged in groups which are sometimes called verses but are more correctly referred to as **stanzas**. This is called **strophic poetry**. Keats uses this form in *The Eve of St Agnes*, as does Blake in *The Tyger* and Ted Hughes in *Crow*, for example.

There are many different kinds of stanza, with variations depending on the number of lines they contain. (See the previous section on rhyme, and the **List of terms** for further descriptions.)

The sonnet

The sonnet is a very popular form in English poetry and it is one that you are likely to come across in your studies. In basic terms a sonnet is a fourteen-line poem and the lines are usually arranged in one of two ways. First, there is the **Petrarchan** or **Italian sonnet** (so called because it is named after the Medieval Italian writer, Petrarch). This kind of sonnet is arranged with a first part that consists of eight lines (the octave) and a second and concluding part of six lines (the sestet). There can be variations in the rhyme scheme but generally it follows: *abbaabba cdecde*.

The other form is the **Shakespearean** or **English sonnet**. The rhyme scheme of this form is divided into three quatrains and a concluding couplet and usually follows the pattern: *abab cdcd efef gg*.

Free verse

Although forms which adhere to a strict pattern are still frequently used by poets in the twenty-first century, there has been a trend towards poetry that does not have the constraints of metre or rhyme upon it, making free verse more predominant. This form of verse often does not have lines that are equal in length or that have a regular metre, and often it does not rhyme. To a large extent this flexibility allows poets the freedom to create forms to suit their own purposes and achieve the effects that they want in their writing.

Thematic form

Certain forms of poetry have been used to express themes which can be broadly grouped together. (This is sometimes called **thematic form**.) For example, the ode, the ballad, the elegy, the aubade, the pastoral, the lyric, the epic, and the song all refer to particular kinds of poetry that have a broad thematic link in common. (See the **List of terms** for more information on specific forms.)

Obviously the form of a poem in terms of its physical structure is inseparably linked to the idea of its thematic form. In turn, the whole concept of form is interlinked with other features such as rhyme, rhythm, and the poet's overall intention. What is important is that you are able to suggest reasons why a poet has chosen a particular form and comment on how it contributes, along with all these other features, in creating the poem's overall effect.

Chaucer's Poetry

Chaucer is generally considered to be the most important writer of the Middle Ages and his work, especially *The Canterbury Tales*, certainly had a great influence on English literature and language, laying the foundations for many writers who came after him. It is no surprise, therefore, to find Chaucer featured on a variety of AS and A Level English Literature specifications. For this specification you will need to compare one of *The Canterbury Tales* to a set drama text.

Reading Middle English

In the initial stages of your study of Chaucer you may encounter problems of understanding that are not present in other types of poetry. When you first open your copy of whichever Chaucer text you are studying, probably the first thing to strike you will be that it appears to be written in another language. Initially, this can be quite unsettling. Do not be put off, though, because once you have become used to the language things will seem much simpler. The language itself is nowhere near as daunting as it can look at first sight.

The first thing to bear in mind is that it is not written in another language – it is very definitely written in English. Admittedly, it is a rather different form of English from our present-day language because it is the English that was used in the fourteenth century. It is called Middle English and evolved as a mixture of different language elements.

French was influential in the development of Middle English since from the time of the Norman Conquest in 1066 until the mid-thirteenth century, it was the language of the court and the upper-middle classes. Latin also made an important contribution to Middle English, being the language of legal and ecclesiastical documents and the preferred language of scholarly communication in the Middle Ages. These elements, combined with the predominant east Midland dialect (the dialect of Chaucer), gradually evolved into Middle English. This is the form of language from which modern English developed. In some respects modern English is similar to Middle English, but there are differences too.

In studying Chaucer for the first time your first task is to become familiar with these similarities and differences. There are a number of things that you can do to help you to quickly become quite fluent in reading Chaucer in the original. Try reading the text out loud, pronouncing each word just as it looks. Write down a 'translation' of the text based on your reading and make a note of any words that puzzle you or cause you a problem in the translation. Following your initial reading, check difficult words in the glossary to your text. Consider researching references to places, people and mythology further, if you feel it will aid your understanding.

As you read you may notice some, or all of the following points:

- Some words are identical to their modern English counterparts (e.g. 'bathed', 'every', 'called', 'loved').
- Some words look and sound very similar to their modern English counterparts (e.g. 'whan', 'greet', 'wonne').
- Some words look completely unfamiliar (e.g. 'soote', 'swich', 'eek').
- Some words might remind you of modern English words but actually mean something different (e.g. 'inspired', 'holt').
- Some of the words seem to be in a strange order.
- There are references to people, places, etc. that you might not have come across before (e.g. 'Zephirus').

The context of the tales

If you decide to study Chaucer as part of your A Level studies it is likely that you will choose one of the poems which make up *The Canterbury Tales*. Whichever particular tale you are studying, though, it is important that you consider the tale in the wider context of *The Canterbury Tales*, rather than just looking at it in isolation. Each of the tales is set within the fictional framework established by Chaucer in the *General Prologue to the Canterbury Tales*, which is a kind of introduction where Chaucer sets the scene and introduces and describes the pilgrims.

The basic background to the tales is straightforward. A group of pilgrims are travelling from London to Canterbury to worship at the shrine of Thomas à Becket. They meet at the Tabard Inn at Southwark in London ready to begin their journey and the landlord, or Host, as he is known, suggests that they all take part in a story-telling competition to help to pass the time on their journey. The Host will judge the stories and the winner will receive a free meal at the inn on their return from Canterbury.

In your edition of the tale that you are studying, you will probably find other material which is not part of the tale itself, but which will help you to establish some background to the character telling the tale. This material usually includes at least two extracts taken from elsewhere in *The Canterbury Tales*:

- most editions contain the section taken from the *General Prologue* which describes the particular pilgrim who is telling the tale
- most editions also contain the relevant lines that link the tale in question to the one that immediately precedes it. This often involves an exchange between the pilgrims and the Host, which can help to throw light on the characters and how they relate to one another.

The narrator's voice

The Canterbury Tales, then, is a story about a group of people telling stories. The characters are, of course, the invention of Chaucer but he also writes himself into the script by taking the role of one of the pilgrims. In fact, in his role as Sir Topas, he gives himself the worst tale of all to tell and is interrupted by the Host who can listen to no more, preventing him from finishing it.

Throughout the tales there is always a sense of the presence of two narrators: firstly the character telling the story but secondly, hidden somewhere behind the first narrator, there is Chaucer himself, masterminding the whole scheme.

Activity

What do you think Chaucer gains by having his tales narrated by fictitious characters within a fictitious framework, rather than simply telling the tales directly himself?

There are several factors that you might consider here:

- The idea of the group of pilgrims gives a sense of unity and structure to what might otherwise have been a loosely linked collection of stories.
- Links can be made between the character telling the tale and the tale itself, adding another dimension to both tale and teller.

- The whole narrative scheme is given a depth and complexity in terms of its overall effect on the audience, that would have been lacking in a simple single narration scheme.

- It allows Chaucer to get away with telling stories and making comments that may be ribald or contentious by distancing himself from them and attributing them to his characters. This can add to the ironic effect he often creates.

In most of the tales, Chaucer remains in the background, but watch out for his voice coming through. Sometimes he will comment or make an aside or observation. Occasionally he will endow a character with a language or mode of expression which is very much his own. In *The Miller's Tale*, Chaucer is able to convince his audience that the Miller is an independent character over whom he has no control, and he urges readers to choose another tale if they are likely to be offended by the Miller's bawdy offering.

The key thing throughout is to be aware of the subtlety with which Chaucer uses a variety of narrative voices to achieve just the effect he wants. Following these steps should help you to tackle your Chaucer text confidently:

- Read the tale you are studying through fairly quickly to get a general sense of what it is about. Do not worry too much at this first stage if there are words, phrases, or sections of it that you do not understand.

- Avoid using your glossary too much during this 'first read' stage. This can interrupt your reading and make it more difficult to get the overall feel of the story.

- Following your first reading, look back over the tale and focus on the individual words, phrases, or sections that gave you problems and use the glossary to help form a picture of their meanings.

- Most editions of a particular tale will contain quite detailed line-referenced notes. Make full use of these – they will help you to establish the meaning of more difficult sections and also fill in some useful background information that will add to your understanding of the tale.

- Try listening to a recording of the tale read by a professional. This will help you to gain an impression of the sound of the language and you will hear rhymes and rhythms that are invisible when looking at the printed page.

- Avoid using a modern English translation. If you go straight to a translation this will prevent you from coming to terms with the language for yourself. It is far better to be able to read the original for yourself than have to rely on a ready-made translation.

Milton's poetry

Milton's use of language is closer to modern English than Chaucer's but his choice of vocabulary and references to the ideas and politics of his time can still be a challenge to students reading his poetry.

Milton lived and wrote in the seventeenth century. During the English Civil War, he eventually sided with the Puritans who were opposed to the rule of Charles I mainly because the king implemented policies to persecute them and to prevent them from worshipping. The Puritans believed that the Church of England still held too many ties with the Roman Catholic Church and wanted further reforms to services and religious practices. Milton became the Secretary for the Foreign Tongues for the Puritans, translating political documents.

He was also a leading author of the Puritan pamphlets which were issued to try to justify Oliver Cromwell's reign and the execution of Charles I.

When set for A Level, work on Milton's poetry will involve the study of one or more books of Milton's epic, *Paradise Lost* (1667), and for this specification you will need to compare this to a set drama text. *Paradise Lost* concerns itself with the fall of Adam and Eve and was originally published in ten books, although later it was issued in twelve books – the traditional number for an epic.

Although he wrote poetry throughout his life, producing various works including *L'Allegro* (1632), *Il Penseroso* (1632), *Comus* (1634), and *Lycidas* (1637), it was in the latter part of his life that his long, or epic, poems like *Paradise Lost* and later *Samson Agonistes* (1671) were written.

When reading Milton for the first time you may come accross the following difficulties:

- Milton's language consists of words that are unfamiliar to you.
- Milton mentions names that you have not heard of before – 'Titanian', 'Briareos', 'Typhon', 'Tarsus' or 'Leviathan', for example.
- The word order is sometimes different from that which you are used to.
- The text appears to consist mainly of description with very little action.

One of the challenges of reading and understanding poetry that was written hundreds of years ago relates to the references or allusions that poets use. While these references would have been understood and would have held some significance to a reader in the poet's own age, they can often mean little to us today. These are not difficulties confined to poetry written a long time ago (a reading of T.S. Eliot's *The Wasteland* will convince you of that), but the chances of encountering them are probably greater the older the poetry is. However, good editions usually contain notes and glossaries to help the reader understand these more obscure references and so appreciate the text fully.

Milton uses many references and allusions to classical literature and to the Bible in his work, and a knowledge of Greek and Roman mythology will help a good deal in studying his poetry. His readers in the seventeenth century would have possessed this kind of background and would have immediately understood these biblical references and classical allusions. For them, the references, would have served, as they were intended to do, to illuminate and illustrate the work. Today, most of us do not have this kind of background, and so often such references can initially act as barriers to meaning rather than assisting our understanding.

The question is – what can you do to help yourself overcome these initial difficulties? Well, three things would help to begin with:

- Buy a good dictionary if you do not possess one already, and use it. Make sure that you look up every word you come across that you do not understand. It can be a good idea to make a list of these.
- Look up and make a note of references that you do not understand. You might need to consult classical websites, dictionaries or encyclopedias for some of these.
- Ask yourself questions. Never be satisfied with ignoring difficult words or references. Always ask yourself questions like 'Why is that reference used?', 'What does it mean?', 'What does it add to the sense or effect of the poem?'

Understanding Milton's imagery

The simile form is an important part of the imagery used in *Paradise Lost*. Some poetic images are drawn on a grand scale and can be elaborate and quite complicated to unravel. The key thing to remember is that often poetry needs working at in order to develop a good understanding of it.

Here are some suggestions to help you with that process:

- Read the piece several times.
- Use the parts of the poetry that you understand as clues to help you work through more difficult sections.
- Highlight particularly difficult words, phrases, lines and images.
- Look up words that you do not understand in a good dictionary.
- Refer to the notes or glossary that the text contains.
- Do some background reading about the writer and his or her period.

The poetry of John Donne

As part of your studies for Unit F663: Drama and Poetry pre-1800, you may have the opportunity to study the poetry of John Donne. Like the poetry of Chaucer, your aim in the exam will be to compare the poetry to your set drama text for this unit. Donne's language is much closer to modern English than Chaucer's, but students approaching his work face challenges of other kinds.

Donne was born in 1572 and died in 1631. During his life he worked as a clergyman, fought as a soldier and became a Member of Parliament. Despite what is known of his life, it is very difficult to directly connect any of his poetry to his personal experiences because most of his work cannot be dated. In fact, most of his work remained in manuscript until after he died.

Whilst reading Donne's poetry in the context of his life is problematic there is, however, much to gain from consideration of the times in which he lived. Today the period in which Donne was writing is referred to as the 'Renaissance'.

As with many of the words we use to indicate periods of culture, 'Renaissance' was only used after the age it describes was over. The term refers to a period of artistic and intellectual activity which began in Italy in the fourteenth century and was influential throughout Europe until the seventeenth century. Donne could not have said: 'I am a Renaissance poet.' Yet he was undoubtedly a poet who displayed a restless, exploratory spirit, which delighted in testing out ideas and questioning many accepted views. He was born into a culture that was re-thinking painting, sculpture, architecture, law, politics, religion, literature, philosophy and science. That culture, at once both exciting and frightening, was Donne's context. Donne's wide range of images in his poetry reflect the fervour of intellectual interest and debate in these subject matters during his day. These subjects include exploration, medical advancement, astronomy, art and religious reform.

Metaphysical poetry

Donne (and later poets such as Herbert, Marvell and Crashaw) is often called a metaphysical poet. The term goes back to the poet John Dryden (1631–1700) who wrote that Donne 'affects the Metaphysics', meaning that he introduces philosophical and scholarly issues into his poems. By the twentieth century, the term came to be used of the features commonly associated with the poetry of Donne and his later followers. Therefore the following points characterize metaphysical poetry:

- There is a dramatic sense of the poet in the poem. The poet is present in striking openings and purposeful arguing.
- The rhythms and sounds of the poem approximate closely to the patterns of everyday speech, marked by outbursts of feeling and thoughtful hesitations.
- There is a conscious delight in intellectual cleverness, often in the form of complex wordplay.
- The attitudes of the poet are often abrasively cynical, bitter, jesting or dismissive.
- There is a love of intricate argument and delight in paradoxes.
- The imagery is drawn from a wide range of academic fields. This gives the poems an intellectual, or scholarly, thrust.
- The images are often outlandish. The reader has to struggle to see the appropriateness of what is being said.

The range of topics is wide, and often several subjects intertwine: in Donne's poems emotions range from the exuberant pleasures of love, to burdened meditations on mortality and sin.

The living voice

Donne sounds like no other poet. This is largely due to his language having the characteristics of everyday speech. In a Donne poem there are:

- quickenings of pace
- clusters of heavy stresses
- surprising cadences or movement of sounds created within the poetry
- sudden changes in tone
- interruptions of rhythmic patterns
- variations in line length
- groupings of monosyllabic words
- short rhyming couplets
- a high proportion of verbs.

F.R. Leavis famously said that we read Donne 'as we read the living'. And a living voice is what we hear – urgent, passionate, purposeful and intellectually engaged.

Drama

Because we hear a living voice in Donne's poem, he has often been compared to a dramatist. Dramatists of the day – Marlowe, Shakespeare, Webster – gave their characters lengthy speeches, which revealed intentions, motivations and turbulent emotional lives. How true is this also of Donne?

Another aspect of the drama of Donne's poems is that they imply a story or narrative leading up to the situation in which the poet speaks. Readers often have to piece together the story and imagine the drama of the situation. The drama of the situation is often strong in the love poems, and though immediate circumstances are less vivid in the religious poems, we are invited to imagine narratives leading to the utterances in Holy Sonnets *13*, *14*, *17* and *19*. The consequences for the reader is that we have to learn to hear the speaker, to put ourselves in the position of the listener and, in some cases, picture the physical circumstances in which the encounter between the speaker and listener takes place.

The narrative element and the immediacy of the encounter explain why Donne's poems are sometimes said to be dramatic monologues. Although this term is usually applied to nineteenth-century poems, such as those by Browning and Tennyson, the defining features of a situation, a person who is addressed and a revelation (not necessarily intentional) of the speaker's motives and mind can be found in some of Donne's poems.

Challenges of Donne's writing

When reading Donne's poetry, or when comparing it to your other set text, you are likely to discover a number of challenging complexities within his work.

- **The conceit:** A conceit is a far-fetched comparison which, surprisingly, draws attention to similarities between apparently very different objects. It was a common feature of sixteenth- and seventeenth-century poetry. At first conceits seem strange or astonishing, but thinking about them reveals some kind of truth

  When reading Donne however, we might sometimes find ourselves saying: this is strange rather than true. What we should remember is that all responses are significant. Those who find truth in Donne's puzzling conceits are committed to saying that he is a poet that tells us something, either about how things are or the human condition. Those who find him strange will have judged the poetry as only revealing what Donne was like.

- **Ambivalence:** Donne's thinking is also ambivalent. The reader is often unclear as to what the tone of the poem is. This makes interpretation a challenge. Is his subject matter sacred or everyday? Is he a poet of reason or feeling? Is he more at home with ideas than with people? Does he play the role of the adventurous lover Jack Donne or Dr Donne the preacher?

  Faced with poems that zigzag in their thought and are ambivalent in their attitudes, it is not easy to sum up their subject matter. We should never forget, however, that different ideas often exist alongside each other within single poems.

- **Ellipses:** Under the pressure of urgent thought, Donne's style often becomes elliptical, meaning that words are omitted. The result often puzzles readers, but beyond puzzlement what most readers sense is his delight. Think about how words that scaffold arguments – 'if', 'but', 'then' – are frequently delivered with an incisive thrust.

- **Biblical References:** Religious language features in many of Donne's poems. As might be expected, the religious poems contain references to the Bible, to Christian tradition and to theology.

  Virtually everybody of Donne's time engaged in public worship, and religious allegiance shaped moral, social and political behaviour. It may be difficult for a twenty-first-century reader to fully engage with the detail of some of Donne's references or the sense of supreme importance that many of these issues bore on the individual consciousness.

  Using a bible dictionary and the notes to your text will provide a helpful insight into some of these issues.

- **The Subject:** A final issue is the problem frequently encountered in Donne: to whom is the poet speaking? The audience of the love poems is the beloved; God is the audience of the religious poems. But to whom is he the more attentive?

The reader may well feel that at times the lover is so fascinated by his own thinking that he forgets his beloved's presence. But does the poet forget God? Might it be that Donne's most intense love poetry is that addressed to God?

Donne the lover, is the figure (or figures) created in the poems. When writing about him, we should always remember that we cannot assume that Donne is talking about his own feelings. The experiences conveyed through the poems are remarkably varied in terms of tone, emotion and the role the poet plays.

Writing about Donne

The following remarks may be useful as you prepare to write about Donne in relation to your set drama text.

- You should try to convey Donne's delight in his ingenious thinking. Try to bring out the art by which he draws the reader into the twists and turns of intellectual debate.

- One of the delights of Donne is the movement of thought and feeling. When we talk about the dramatic quality of his verse, one of the things we are drawing attention to is the way each poem is a kind of story, a series of emotional or intellectual events that add up to something of interest and importance.

- When writing about Donne, try to bring out the range of his learning and the purpose to which he puts it. Remember that learning often shows something about how people think and feel.

- Never forget that he is a poet of his times. The excitement of learning in an age when knowledge was uncertain gives a dangerous edge to what he writes.

- It is a good idea to handle the critical language associated with Donne. Words such as 'conceit' and 'metaphysical' can help us think through what Donne's work is like.

- Donne's verse is characterised by verbal music. The exquisite blends of sounds in a line are not only beautiful but enact the thoughts and feelings of the words.

- Remember that there are many moods in Donne. He can be darkly serious as well as funny. Readers might find the religious poems more personal than those above human love.

- Finally, never forget your own responses. Donne is a writer who provokes us into engaging with his ways of thinking and feeling, so what you feel about him is an important part of that engagement.

The poetry of Alexander Pope

If you choose to study Alexander Pope for Unit F633, you will focus on Pope's mock epic poem, *The Rape of the Lock*. Your aim in the exam will be to compare and contrast this poem with a set drama text.

Alexander Pope was born in 1688, the year of the Glorious Revolution when James II fled to France in the face of civil riots against his Roman Catholicism; and William and Mary were invited to become Protestant rulers of England. Three years after this in 1701, the Act of Settlement was passed, which meant that all future heirs to the throne had to be Protestant.

Alexander Pope's parents were both Roman Catholic and Pope continued in this faith all his life, despite the legal restrictions and civil disadvantages which Catholics suffered after 1688. As a Roman Catholic, Pope could not attend university; he could not hold public office or practise a profession; he could not own property or live within ten miles of London. He was taxed double, besides having to follow many rules such as not being allowed to own fire-arms or a horse worth more than five pounds.

When Pope was about thirteen he caught a disease which is thought to have been a form of spinal tuberculosis. It left him physically deformed. He never grew taller than four and a half feet. His body became twisted and hunchbacked and the effort of standing and moving created chords of tension which stood out in his face in later life. His enemies, and there were many later in his life, used his physical deformities to attack him: 'a crooked mind in a crooked body'; 'a little monster'; 'hunchback'd toad'; 'ape'; 'grinning monkey' are only a few of the things he was called. Pope claimed indifference, and gave as good as he got in his own writings, but tellingly, he kept records of these personal attacks, gathering them into four bound volumes.

The context of the poem

Besides mastering technical excellence, Pope believed that a poet should act as a moral leader: someone who commented on the world rather than engaging with it, and who, from the vantage point of self-chosen retirement from public life, was a leading spokesperson for the age. In *The Rape of the Lock* for example, Pope reveals the vanity and self-importance of the people of fashionable eighteenth-century society.

The occasion of the poem was a quarrel between two land-owning Roman Catholic families, the Petres and the Fermors. We know only the barest details of the incident from Pope himself.

Arabella Fermor was a society beauty whose good looks had been celebrated in verse by several poets. Lord Petre was a young aristocrat who had inherited his estate in his teens under the guardianship of John Caryll. Pope barely knew Arabella. He never met Lord Petre. The Carylls were his friends and it was John Caryll, the 'common acquaintance', who was the real instigator of the poem.

The youth of the characters suggests a romantic affair, but if it was so, the courtship was short-lived. Before the poem was published Lord Petre was married, and not to Arabella who wed a Berkshire gentleman a few years later.

The Rape of the Lock exists in three distinct versions. In answer to Caryll's request, Pope wrote his first two-canto poem quickly in 1711 and circulated it privately to the parties concerned. He published it in 1712 in *Miscellaneous Poems and Translations*, a collection of poems by various poets. In 1714 Pope published the longer five-canto version, introducing 'the Machinery' (the band of aerial beings) and adding a number of mock-epic incidents. The third version was for Pope's collected *Works* 1717 when he added Clarissa's speech in Canto V, 'to open more clearly the moral of the poem', he explained.

The style of the poem

When Pope set out to please Caryll by writing something to 'laugh' the quarrelling families 'together again' he chose to write a mock-epic and this decision determined the style of his poem. The mock-epic is a particular type of poem recognized by its use of heroic language and references to classical Greek and Roman literature, which are used in the context of a rather trivial or 'everyday' subject matter. The style of the mock-epic is a challenge in itself to modern readers who may lack the background to recognize classical allusions with ease.

Much of the humour and witty effect of the poem however, can be appreciated through careful attention to tone. At what points does the tone change from epic to conversational? The 'epic' tone of Pope's writing can be identified in a number of ways, such as through Pope's use of language, verse structure and rhyme.

Language

Pope uses the standard epic formula of a noun accompanied by an adjective which is elevated and inexact in meaning. It is easy to find examples of Pope using features of epic style from 'dire offense' and 'mighty contests' to 'verdant fields' and 'smoaking tyde'.

The Rape of the Lock is full of phrases where what is intended by the adjective is slightly mysterious: 'secret passions', 'grateful liquors', 'two-edg'd weapon', 'fatal shears'. The choice of inflated words and the association of nouns with adjectives grand in tone and vague in meaning are features of the epic and the mock-epic. In the mock-epic, the reader may feel surprise when they realize the unimportance of the object highlighted by the grandiose ring of the phrase which describes it. A 'two-edg'd weapon' sounds ferocious until one remembers that it is a pair of scissors so tiny that the Baron can hardly fit them on the ends of his fingers.

Rhythm and rhyme

The Rape of the Lock is written in the rhythm of iambic pentameter. You may have come across this term at GCSE level, but to recap, iambic pentameter is the term used to describe lines consisting of ten syllables divided into five, two-syllable units known as 'feet'. The second syllable of each iambic 'foot' is stressed. A rhymed pair of iambic pentameters is called a heroic couplet and this is the style in which Pope wrote the poem.

The iambic pentameter and the closing of each couplet with a rhyme mean that Pope is writing in a highly restrictive mode. The formal restraints of his chosen style mirror the world of artifice and decorum which his poem describes. Amidst these expected rhymes Pope slips in some which lower the tone, mocking and undercutting the epic mode; 'mankind'/'behind'; 'bestow'/'Furbelow'; 'brocade'/'masquerade'; 'fail'/'whale'. The joke lies in the oddity of the pairing.

Structure

Pope often structures his verse paragraphs so that the shift between the epic and the trivial occurs at specific, dramatic moments in the verse. This often occurs at the end of a paragraph, for example. How does this influence the effect of the change in tone? Is the joke at the end heightened by the build-up which precedes it? Once recognized, you will begin to find further instances of Pope building paragraphs towards mocking conclusions. Some verse paragraphs also move in the opposite direction.

Poetic devices

Pope also uses various established poetic methods of writing in a comical and belittling manner.

- **Bathos:** A sudden shift of tone which produces a comical effect by means of an unexpected descent from exalted content and language to the banal or the 'ordinary'. For example, in the line stating that great Anna, 'Dost sometimes counsel take – and sometimes Tea', content moves from important state business, 'counsel', to simple behaviour, taking 'Tea', so rapidly that the effect is startling and amusingly discordant.

Bathos is a diminishing comic device which Pope uses throughout the poem to poke fun at his characters' inflated sense of their own importance, yet he uses it ambiguously.

- **Zeugma:** The technical term given to a device Pope uses frequently in *The Rape of the Lock*. A single verb governs two objects and is used in a different sense in each case, for example, in the lines quoted above, that great Anna 'dost sometimes counsel take–and sometimes Tea'–where advice and a cup of tea are both proper objects of the verb 'to take' but read incongruously when used at the same time.

  Pope's use of zeugma seems to go to the heart of his mocking and ambiguous attitude towards Belinda and reflects her judgement of her world. There is a sense that, if not to the reader then at least to Anna and Sir Plume, the incongruously different objects are of equal importance. If Queen Anne takes counsel in the spirit in which she drinks tea, what does this imply about the seriousness with which she treats state business?

- **Irony:** The humorous or mildly sarcastic use of words to imply the opposite of what, on the surface, is intended. The Baron's apparent compliment to Sir Plume as someone 'Who speaks so well' is ironic, since it is clear that Sir Plume's stumbling request to return the curl is the opposite of speaking 'well'. You might like to consider the meaning, overt and implied, of 'strange', 'three garters', 'maladies', 'no more', and to look yourself for further instances of Pope's undercutting of surface meaning with subtly judgemental irony.

- **Satire:** A literary form dating from the classical period in which events and issues, usually contemporary and often political, are attacked by being held up to witty ridicule. Pope would not himself have called *The Rape of the Lock* a satire because to him the comic elements of exaggeration, bathos and irony are part of the mock-heroic, a gentler form of mockery which contrasts high epic ideals with less heroic contemporary life. It is however a term commonly applied by later critics to the way in which the poem ridicules and belittles the fashionable world of beaux and belles obsessed with 'trivial things'.

Studying drama

What is drama?

A dictionary definition will state that:

> Drama is something intended specifically for performance on stage in front of an audience.

This definition points to the fact that drama is written to be seen rather than read, and its meaning can only be fully appreciated when seen in performance. This makes it a much more public form of literature than prose or poetry, in that the experience of the play in performance is a shared experience. This essential aspect of drama is easy to lose sight of when sitting in a classroom, or on your own, grappling with the language of a drama text.

Visualizing the script

It is essential when approaching a play that you are aware you are dealing with a work that is very different from, say, a novel and that you will need to employ quite different strategies to handle it. You must be able to visualize the play in your head – be able to bring the play alive in your mind and see and hear the action as if you were at the theatre. Developing the ability to do this can be difficult simply by reading from the printed page. However, there are things you can do, from the outset, to help.

• Recognize that reading a play is essentially a group activity and so work with others as much as possible.

• Go to see plays performed as often as possible. (Do not restrict yourself to the ones you are studying, or just to professional productions.)

• Keep a notebook or log of plays that you see, noting your responses – thoughts and feelings about performances and ideas on production.

• Take part in acting out parts of a play – this will help you to appreciate the staging implications of a text in a way that straight reading never can.

• Listen to audio or watch video recordings of plays. (These do not replace seeing the play live but they are better than only reading the script.)

With all of this in mind, let us consider some aspects of plays that you will need to examine in the texts that you study.

Opening scenes

The way that a play opens is obviously crucial to engaging the audience's attention, and writers can take many options here depending on the effects that they wish to achieve. In looking at an opening scene, whether of a text you are studying for an exam or coursework, there are some key questions that are worth asking. The central questions are: 'What effect does the writer want this scene to have on the audience?' and 'What purpose does the scene serve to the play as a whole?'. Here are some possible answers to these questions.

• The scene provides an explanation of background information and details that the audience needs in order to understand what is going on. (This is sometimes called **exposition**.)

• The scene creates a setting or background against which the play is set.

• The scene creates a mood or creates tension which captures the audience's attention immediately (the opening scene of *Hamlet* is a good example of this).

• The scene introduces characters, situations, and relationships.

• The scene provokes a sense of intrigue which captures the audience's attention and makes them want to know more.

Presenting character

A key element in the impact of a dramatic production is the extent to which the playwright achieves a convincing sense of character. However, the nature of drama is such that the playwright employs very different methods of characterization from those employed by a novelist. Novelists can provide the reader with as much background information as they wish. They can enter the minds of the characters, let their readers know what characters think, feel and are planning to do. A playwright does not have all these options.

Perhaps the most straightforward way in which a playwright can define exactly how he or she intends a character to appear to the audience is through detailed and explicit stage directions. So it is important that when you begin to study a play that you pay close attention to this information. When watching the play on the stage, you will not be reading stage directions but you will be seeing them in performance.

Some playwrights provide little direct guidance on how to interpret their characters but rely on other methods to convey a sense of character. These include:

- how characters speak (also embedded in stage directions)
- how characters are described by other characters
- what the characters say and do.

Most playwrights use a combination of all these methods in order to give a sense of fully developed characters, although in some cases playwrights deliberately create stereotypical characters in order to achieve a particular effect. Some of the stock characters to be found in Restoration comedy, or a comedy of manners such as *The Rivals* by Richard Sheridan, are examples of this.

Asides and soliloquies

To succeed in creating a convincing character, the dramatist needs to give the audience some sense of deeper, inner thoughts and feelings. Unlike the novelist, who can describe these as fully as desired to the reader, the dramatist has much more limited means at his or her disposal.

Two methods often used to provide insight into characters' minds are the aside and the soliloquy. The **aside** is a kind of stage whisper, a behind-the-hand comment. Sometimes it is directed to another character but often it is aimed at the audience or characters appear to 'speak to themselves'. Asides tend to be short, often a single sentence, sometimes a single word. They are used by the playwright to convey small pieces of information concerning the plot or character to the audience. For example, in William Congreve's *The Way of the World* one of the central characters, Mirabell, has insincerely courted Lady Wishfort as a cover for his real love of her niece, Millamant. Lady Wishfort has discovered the truth and, although she gives nothing away in conversation, her aside shows that despite Mirabell's deceit she is still susceptible to his charms.

Lady Wishfort: *(Aside)* Oh, he has witchcraft in his eyes and tongue! When I did not see him, I could have bribed a villain to his assassination; but his appearance rakes the embers which have so long lain smothered in my breast.

Although asides are usually short comments, sometimes they can be more extended. In Richard Sheridan's, *The Rivals* the characters almost give the audience a running commentary on what is going on and how they are feeling. It is also worth noting that lines which can be taken as asides in performance are not always marked *(Aside)* in the script.

The aside is an extremely useful device by which the playwright can give hints concerning plot or character to the audience. Through the **soliloquy**, the playwright has much more scope for developing a character's thoughts and feelings aloud, allowing the audience to see into the mind of the character. The soliloquy is an expanded and more fully developed speech and is usually delivered when the character is alone on the stage. Often soliloquies allow characters to reveal the feelings, plans, or motives that they are compelled to conceal in front of the other characters.

Soliloquies frequently appear at a special moment in the play or when a character is undergoing some kind of emotionally or psychologically heightened experience. For example, it could be when a character is distressed or suffering a confusion of mind, or alternatively when a character wants to work through his or her own thoughts and feelings.

Although, technically speaking, we expect a character to be alone on the stage, or out of earshot of other characters when they deliver their soliloquy, a soliloquy-like effect can be created in other ways. Sometimes characters may be in the presence of others, but they are so wrapped up in their own world that it is as though they are talking to themselves. Although this is not strictly a soliloquy, it can serve much the same function.

It has often been noted that both the aside and the soliloquy are artificial devices and that in real life people do not go around delivering speeches to themselves. In fact, they are just two of many conventions that we accept when watching a play, which can be regarded as dramatic licence. In the context of the theatre we forget their artificiality and accept them quite naturally.

Activity

1 Working in pairs, select a character from a play that you are studying. One assumes the role of that character, the other the mirror image. The character asks questions of the image about thoughts, feelings and motivations, and the image answers. This role play should teach you as much about what your chosen character is not as what he or she is.

2 You can then select another character and swap roles.

Issues and themes

Complex though the formation and development of characters may be, they are themselves part of a more intricate web that makes up the play as a whole. Within this web the playwright will have interwoven certain themes and issues. In studying a play, you will need to be able to identify these and to look at how the playwright explores them through the drama. Such ideas can be presented to the audience in two key ways. First, we can detect ideas, issues and thoughts expressed by the characters in a play. Secondly, we can detect themes, issues, or ideas that the playwright wants the play as a whole to project.

Sometimes a playwright will make major characters hold views or follow a philosophy that ultimately is shown to contradict the message that the play as a whole conveys. This is often done to show the problems caused by, or shortcomings of, certain courses of action or philosophies. The issues that a play might raise can be many and varied but they are almost always presented via action based upon human relationships and conflicts.

Plot and structure

Plot is central to most plays, although there are certain kinds of play (some of Samuel Beckett's, for example) where the very lack of a plot, or at least something that we would ordinarily recognize as a plot, is essential for the effect. At its simplest, the **plot** is the story of the play – what happens. Having said that, there is much more to plot than simple story-line. The whole notion of plot and its development is bound up with the way that the play is put together; with its structure. The creation of an order or pattern requires careful planning and the playwright needs to consider a number of factors. Generally speaking an effective plot should:

- maintain the interest of the audience from beginning to end
- move the action on from one episode to the next
- arouse the interest of the audience in character and situation
- create high points or moments of crisis at intervals
- create expectation and surprise.

Usually, the structure of a play follows a basic pattern which consists of a number of identifiable elements.

1 **Exposition:** This opens the play and often introduces the main characters and provides background information.

2 **Dramatic incitement:** This is the incident which provides the starting point for the main action of the play.

3 **Complication:** This usually forms the main action of the play, as the characters respond to the dramatic incitement and other developments that stem from it.

4 **Crisis:** This is the climax of the play.

5 **Resolution:** This is the final section of the play where things are worked out and some kind of conclusion is arrived at.

Sub-plots

Sub-plots are secondary plots, sometimes separate from the main action but often linked to it in some way. Sub-plots tend to echo themes explored by the main plot or shed more light on them. They contribute to the interest of the play but do not detract from the main plot.

The pace of the action is also integral to the idea of plot and structure. Varying the pace at which the plot unfolds is another factor in maintaining the interest of the audience. Variations in the lengths of scenes and in mood, setting and action can all influence a play's dramatic effectiveness.

Approaching your script

There are a number of things you can do to deepen your understanding of a drama text you are studying. Here are some suggestions.

Plays in performance

- See a live performance of the play.
- Failing that, see a video recording of a performance or a film adaptation of it.
- Make notes on performances in a play log book to help you to remember those important initial impressions.
- Read your drama text thoroughly before seeing it performed.
- Listen to the play on audio tape.
- See as many other plays as you can to broaden your experience of drama and the theatre.

Directing the text

- Work with others, dramatizing for yourselves scenes from the text.
- Talk to others about staging implications.
- Imagine you are a director – plan carefully how you would stage a production of the play, the kind of actors you would cast and how you would bring out your own interpretation on the stage.
- Use diagrams, drawings and models to work out sets, stage layout, and props for selected scenes.

Studying the text

- Think about the characters – look at key speeches, look for shifts in focus and different ways of interpreting what they do and say.
- Look for various possible meanings and patterns in the play.
- Consider how/if the theatrical effects are signalled.
- Think about the pace and variety of the action.
- Think about the overall shape and structure of the play and the impact that this could have on an audience.
- Consider the particular characteristics and qualities of the play you are studying.
- Think about relationships between these various elements of the play and how together they present a whole.
- Apply the broader knowledge you have about the nature of plays and drama.

All these activities will help you to formulate and develop your own informed critical response to the play, and therefore fulfil the objectives which lie at the heart of your study of drama.

Shakespeare's drama

Shakespeare has always held a dominant position in the drama element of English Literature at AS and A Level. By the time you reach this stage in your studies you will probably have encountered several Shakespeare plays already. It is likely that you will have studied Shakespeare for Key Stage 3 and Key Stage 4, so you will already be aware of some of the features that characterize his plays.

Since Shakespeare is a dramatist, it follows that his plays have a great deal in common with those of other dramatists.

They follow the clear structural pattern that we discussed earlier:

EXPOSITION → DRAMATIC INCITEMENT → COMPLICATION → CRISIS → RESOLUTION

Similarly, Shakespeare's plays also make use of sub-plots or secondary plots which, although separate from the main action, link with it in some way.

Approaching your text

In approaching the Shakespeare text you are studying, make use of the knowledge you already possess as to the nature of drama generally. This knowledge will help you understand the plot of your Shakespeare text when reading it for the first time. For example, it will help if you know that Shakespeare's plays follow this pattern:

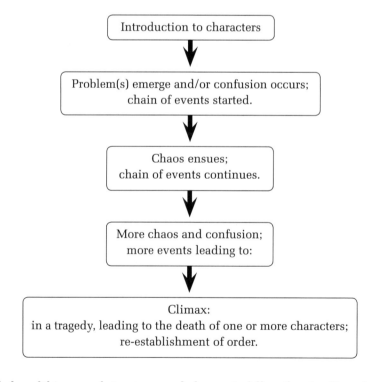

Knowledge of this general structure can help you to follow the storyline of any play, but more than this, it can provide you with a framework for your analysis of the play as a whole. One of the problems that students frequently encounter when studying a Shakespeare text is that they focus so closely on detailed summaries of scene, character and theme that they sometimes lose sight of the fact that the play is an integrated whole. Being able to see the play in terms of its overall framework can help you to appreciate the broad pattern of the text, thus helping you to make sense of the detail when it emerges through more detailed study.

Shakespeare's plays

There are various ways in which the plays of Shakespeare can be categorized, but a useful and straightforward method is to divide them into histories, tragedies and comedies. The texts most frequently studied for AS and A Level are as follows:

Histories	Tragedies	Comedies
Richard II	*Hamlet*	*The Taming of the Shrew*
Henry IV (Part 1)	*Macbeth*	*Love's Labour's Lost*
Henry IV (Part 2)	*Othello*	*A Midsummer Night's Dream*
Henry V	*King Lear*	*Much Ado About Nothing*
Richard III	*Romeo and Juliet*	*The Merchant of Venice*
Antony and Cleopatra		*As You Like It*
Coriolanus		*Twelfth Night*
Julius Caesar		

In addition, there are two further categories for a handful of plays that do not fit easily into the three broad areas.

Problem comedies	Romances
Troilus and Cressida	*Cymbeline*
All's Well That Ends Well	*The Winter's Tale*
Measure for Measure	*The Tempest*

Let's have a closer look at some of the features of plays in each of these categories.

The histories

The main history plays that you are likely to encounter in studying English at AS or A Level are *Richard II*, *Henry IV Part 1*, *Henry IV Part 2*, *Henry V*, and *Richard III*, all of which focus on a specific period of English history. Added to these five are the Roman history plays, *Coriolanus*, *Julius Caesar*, and *Antony and Cleopatra*. It appears that Shakespeare was the first playwright to write a real history play and to treat his material as a drama rather than a mere chronicle of events. His development of character, ideas and themes in these plays makes them far more than simple chronicles, because he adapts historical facts to suit his dramatic purpose.

Although each of Shakespeare's histories is very different from the others in many respects, they do have certain features in common. For example, history plays usually:

- present famous historical figures at moments of crisis in their lives
- concern themselves with the order and stability of the state
- portray rebels who create problems
- have heroes who are fallible
- examine the gap between an ideal notion of kingship and the less tidy reality
- accept the inevitability of disorder
- show that the failings and ambitions of individuals can disrupt the social order.

> ### Activity
> If you are studying a history play, think about these points and decide how many of them you can identify in it. Make a note of how each feature can be seen in your play.

The tragedies

The idea of disorder also lies at the heart of the tragedies. The Roman history plays are often included in the list of tragedies. The four plays that are regarded as the great tragedies are *Hamlet*, *King Lear*, *Othello*, and *Macbeth*. These plays are very frequently set for study at A Level. At the heart of each of these plays is the central character after whom the play is named – the **eponymous hero**, to give the technical term – and the action focuses very much on this character. However, other characters are important too, and often several innocent victims are claimed before the play reaches its end.

Overall, Shakespeare's tragedies have many of the key features we associate with the concept of dramatic tragedy in general.

- At the beginning of the play something occurs that disrupts the normal order of things.
- Chaos or disorder in society results.
- Extreme emotions are involved.
- Social restraint disintegrates.

A climax is reached, usually with the death of the main character (and several others) before order is restored. The purging of emotions that affects the audience at the end of a tragedy is sometimes referred to as **catharsis**.

> ### Activity
> If you are studying one of Shakespeare's tragedies, think about how the play fits this general pattern. Note down one thing that happens in the play which corresponds to each of the above features.

The comedies

The term 'comedy' in modern usage tends to be associated with something fairly lightweight that makes us laugh. However, in its original sense, and certainly as applied to the plays of Shakespeare, the term simply means a play that has a happy ending. The action that leads to this ending may be funny and light in tone, but equally it could deal with serious, even dangerous and life-threatening situations. Shakespearean comedy can deal with issues that are just as serious as those raised by other kinds of plays.

Shakespeare's comedies vary considerably both in style and the mood the play creates. Early comedies such as *The Taming of the Shrew*, *Love's Labour's Lost*, *A Midsummer Night's Dream*, and *Much Ado About Nothing*, or the later comedies, *As You Like It* and *Twelfth Night*, might reasonably be called romantic comedies, as love is a central theme in them. The general pattern for these comedies is as follows:

- life is going on as normal
- characters fall in love
- various mishaps and misunderstandings threaten the happy outcome
- the problems are resolved
- the play ends happily with the various lovers united.

However, in some comedies – notably *Much Ado About Nothing* – a lot of action in the play verges on the tragic and in some ways is reminiscent of *Romeo & Juliet*. This serious edge is clearly apparent in *The Merchant of Venice* too, so much so that the term tragicomedy has been applied to it. The basic pattern, then, is very similar to that of the tragedies:

- an event occurs
- this leads to disorder and disruption
- confusion results
- the problems are resolved.

The difference comes in the way that the action is resolved and the focus that is maintained. In a comedy, serious issues may be raised and addressed but the focus is very much on the foolishness of human behaviour, and the audience usually feels confident that all will turn out well. However, within this structure evil influences may be at work and the play may deal with the powerful negative forces that motivate characters – sexual appetite, lust for power, greed and envy. These forces are nowhere more evident than in the problem comedies.

The problem comedies

Generally, the problem comedies are taken to be *Measure for Measure*, *Troilus and Cressida*, and *All's Well That Ends Well*. In many ways these plays fall somewhere between tragedy and comedy – they avoid becoming tragic because they end happily, at least in so far as no one dies at the end of the play. They are also known as the **problem plays** or **dark comedies**.

A dark tone and flawed characters are typical of these plays. They are more likely to disturb the audience than amuse them, as they raise unsettling issues about the darker side of human nature. Like the other types of plays we have looked at, they centre on disorder within society, but whereas the comedies operate in a world of fantasy and make-believe, these plays take place in a very much bleaker and often coldly realistic environment.

It has been said that in writing these plays Shakespeare was experimenting with a dramatic form which brought together comedy and tragedy. If this is so, his experimentation culminated in the romance plays, written towards the end of his career.

The romance plays

The romances (or 'last plays'), *Pericles*, *Cymbeline*, *The Winter's Tale*, and *The Tempest*, are once again concerned with the idea of disorder. Unlike the problem comedies, which have a harshly realistic setting, these plays make much use of fantasy elements and magic to explore their central ideas. They operate in make-believe worlds and the plots often take improbable or incredible turns and twists. However, these features of the plays are essential to the effects that they create and the purpose they hope to achieve.

Certain key ideas can be seen emerging through all four of these plays:

- the play centres on a noble family and a king
- an evil or misguided deed is done
- this causes great suffering to characters and they endure years of separation
- through the suffering, something new and positive begins to emerge
- in the end this new element transforms the old evil
- an act of forgiveness resolves the problems, and reconciliation takes place.

In simple terms the general pattern can be seen as:

PROSPERITY → DESTRUCTION → RE-CREATION

In many ways the unusual (sometimes bizarre) events that occur in the romances can present added difficulties when you are trying to establish the plot and characters in your mind. However, at their heart are the same features that are present in the other kinds of plays we have discussed. There is order versus disorder; love and harmony versus conflict and discord; and life falling short of the ideal because of human imperfection.

Activity

What type of Shakespeare play are you studying? Draw up a table of the key events and describe the plot structure, thinking about the overall pattern that is created.

Shakespeare's plots

As we have seen, the plots of Shakespeare's plays adhere to a general pattern common to many plays. However, when studying your text, one of the first things you will need to do is to get to grips with the details of the plot. Very often your first encounter with the play will be through a reading, perhaps in class, with students taking the various parts. When reading the play either to yourself or as part of a group, though, it is easy to lose sight of the fact that you are studying a drama. The text you are reading was written to be performed and therefore brought to life on the stage.

Although we now read Shakespeare's plays as literary texts, we must not forget this central fact, and you should view the text as a script. A script suggests something that in itself is incomplete because it needs a dramatic enactment to achieve its purpose. This opens up the whole question of how the play is to be enacted, and touches on the fact that the play has many meanings rather than a single meaning.

In coming to terms with the plot of a Shakespeare play, you first need to understand generally what is happening, and then think about ways in which this could be enacted on the stage. To help you appreciate the variety of ways that a play can be interpreted, you should try to see as many performances of it (live in the theatre, on film, or video) as you can.

Activity

In ten sentences, summarize the plot of the Shakespeare play you are studying. Then take the opening scene of that play and describe two possible, but contrasting, ways in which that scene could be enacted on the stage.

Structure

The structure of each play is integral to the way in which Shakespeare's work develops its central issues. The structure of his plays (or any play) can be viewed in two ways. What is sometimes called the **dynamic structure** of the play consists of the sequence of events which builds up in a 'cause and effect' fashion to create the plot of the play, and so drive the play forward.

Underlying this obvious structure, however, it is often possible to detect another that is less prominent but just as important. This second structure consists of various parallels and cross-references, or repeated images, symbols, and language that create a network of threads running through the play. This kind of structure is sometimes called the **symmetric structure**, and it can exert a powerful influence on the overall effect of a play.

In *Hamlet*, for example, the repeated parallels between Hamlet and Laertes as avenging sons, and Hamlet's repeated contemplation of death with its associated imagery, are just two elements that help to form a web of patterning developed throughout the play. Similarly, in *King Lear*, the theme of 'blindness' to the truth as well as physical blindness, presented through Gloucester and Lear, create parallels that give another kind of structure to the play.

Activity

Draw two diagrams, one to represent the dynamic structure of the Shakespeare play you are studying, the other to represent the symmetric structure.

Character in Shakespeare's plays

An essential part of the study of any play will be to look at the characters and Shakespeare's methods of creating and presenting them.

To put it simply, Shakespeare uses three main techniques to create characters. They reveal themselves:

- through their actions
- by what others say about them
- through their own language.

Activity

Choose one of the central characters from the Shakespeare play that you are studying. Imagine that you are an actor who has been offered that part in a forthcoming production. Collect evidence from the play to support your view of the character and the way that you intend to play the role on stage. Your evidence should consist of the following:

- what the character says about himself or herself
- what others say about the character
- what the character does when speaking
- what the character does when silent
- how the character's words match his or her actual deeds or underlying motives
- how the character is viewed by other characters.

This activity should help you to form your own view of a character. Remember, though, that there is more than one way of looking at a character. Characters in plays, like all other aspects of literature, can rarely be seen in clear-cut, black-and-white terms. As part of your preparation for writing about your play, it would be useful for you to make notes on each of the characters in the play you are studying, making sure that you cover the points in the following list:

- consider all possible interpretations of the character
- assess the role or function that the character performs in the play
- examine in detail the key speeches the character makes and the scenes in which he or she appears
- gather a range of evidence from the play to support your view of the character.

Soliloquies and asides

In most of his plays, Shakespeare makes full use of asides and soliloquies as a means of developing aspects of character.

In Shakespeare's *Othello* there is substantial use of both long and short asides. Often they reveal to the audience the wicked plan developing in Iago's mind, giving a glimpse into his thoughts and the delight he takes in his evil intentions.

Soliloquies, too, are used extensively to convey both information and inward emotion to the audience. In *Hamlet*, for example, it is possible to trace the development of Hamlet's shifting emotions during the course of the play through the sequence of soliloquies he delivers at various points in the action. In *Henry IV Part 1*, Shakespeare uses the dramatic device of the soliliquey to reveal the noble qualities of Prince Hal to the audience. For the course of the play he is regarded as a complete disappointment to his father, King Henry, and all the responsible authority figures in the play, because of his wild and dissolute lifestyle: living in the company of an old reprobate, Falstaff, and his dubious tavern companions. In his soliliquy, Henry reveals that he is very much in control of his conduct and has intentions to reform his character. The audience is therefore allowed to see him in a light that none of the characters can see.

The soliloquy is one key way in which Shakespeare lets us, the audience, know what a character is really like. Through the vehicle of a soliloquy, characters can inform the audience about a whole range of issues, such as what is in their minds, why they are acting the way they are and what they intend to do in the future.

Activity

Look at the play you are studying. Make a list of the soliloquies in it and what those soliloquies tell you about the characters who speak them.

Shakespeare's themes and ideas

Each of Shakespeare's plays is concerned with certain ideas or issues that recur and develop as the play progresses. These topics with which the play is preoccupied are the play's 'themes'. They are the subject that Shakespeare explores through the events, characters and language of the play. It is the themes that create a shape or pattern in the play and give it a significance beyond the events it describes.

The themes are developed through the language of the play, and often Shakespeare creates powerful images. For example, in *Othello* one of the themes of the play is honesty and Iago's dishonesty. The language itself draws attention to this theme in a variety of ways, one of which is the repetition of the word 'honest' to emphasize Othello's complete belief in Iago's honesty and Desdemona's dishonesty.

It has often been said that one of the reasons that Shakespeare's plays have remained popular for so long, lies in the fact that they deal with universal themes that were of concern to people in Shakespeare's time, and are of no less significance to us today. His plays often deal with themes such as love, hate, envy, jealousy, death, revenge, guilt, corruption and destiny.

Certain themes seem to have particularly interested Shakespeare and can be seen in one form or another in all of his plays. These themes are:

* conflict
* appearance and reality
* order and disorder
* change
* love.

Conflict

Conflict, of one type or another, is the starting point for many dramas and it can take many forms. In *Othello*, for example, we have the conflict between Iago and Othello (a conflict that Othello is unaware of until it is too late), and the inner conflict that Othello experiences as he battles to control his growing jealousy. In *Henry IV Part 2*, conflict exists externally as Henry faces rebellion.

Appearance and reality

In all of Shakespeare's plays there is a conflict between how things seem to be and how they actually are. In *Othello*, for example, everyone thinks Iago is 'honest' but in fact he is completely the opposite. In *Twelfth Night*, Viola disguises herself as a boy, while in *Hamlet* the apparently popular and effective King Claudius, is in reality guilty of the murder of his brother and seduction of his brother's wife. In *Measure for Measure* the central theme is the idea of 'seeming'. The Duke leaves his apparently incorruptible deputy, Angelo, in charge of the state, to see 'If power change purpose, what our seemers be'. He discovers the truth about Angelo, when it is revealed that Angelo attempted to seduce the innocent Isabella.

Order and disorder

Shakespeare's plays often feature a breakdown of order, and some form of confusion temporarily gains the upper hand. Sometimes the breakdown is in the order of the state, as in *Macbeth*, where the murder of Duncan plunges the state into turmoil and war. In *Henry IV* (Parts 1 and 2), King Henry faces rebellion and civil war, while *Twelfth Night* begins with Olivia's rejection of Orsino's suit and Viola shipwrecked on the coast of Illyria. The causes of the disruption vary from play to play, but they tend to include key emotions such as jealousy, love, hate, and ambition. Very often the protagonist undergoes some kind of learning process during the course of the play before order is re-established.

Change

In Shakespeare's plays the characters often undergo some kind of change. Sometimes the ultimate result of this change is death, as in *Othello*, for example. Othello changes from a respected military leader to a man eaten away by jealousy, who murders his wife and then, realizing the terrible mistake he has made, takes his own life. In *Twelfth Night*, Malvolio changes from a puritan figure into a foolish lover.

Love

For Shakespeare, one of the instruments of change is love, which has a transforming power and is often at the heart of his plays. *Twelfth Night* begins with the words 'If music be the food of love, play on'. It goes on to present a world of romantic love. In *A Midsummer Night's Dream* we see young men and women who love each other but who also have to endure frustrations in love. In *Othello* we see a quite different portrayal of love, as Othello's love for Desdemona is corrupted into jealousy and hate by the scheming Iago.

Development of themes

Of course, there are many specific themes that can be traced in individual plays, but in one way or another they will relate to the four key areas discussed above.

The themes in Shakespeare's plays often develop in one of three ways:

- An individual character or characters experience some personal difficulties or inner turmoil, perhaps moral or spiritual, that cause mental conflict. For example, Hamlet struggles between coming to terms with events and avenging his father.
- The family, society, or the country is affected by turmoil. For example, the feuding Capulets and Montagues disrupt Verona in *Romeo & Juliet*, and Rome is at war with Egypt in *Antony and Cleopatra*.
- Nature or the universe may be in disorder, or supernatural events may be involved. Examples are the appearance of the witches and Banquo's ghost in *Macbeth*, or the storm imagery in *King Lear*.

At the heart of the development of the themes in each play is Shakespeare's rich and complex use of language.

Shakespeare's language

Often students encounter difficulties when first studying a Shakespeare play because they find the language different in a number of ways from the kind of English they are used to. This difficulty is particularly evident when reading the text rather than watching the play being performed, when actions are brought to life and give the words much more meaning.

At first, concentrate on arriving at a broad understanding of what is happening, in terms of the plot of the play. Once this basic knowledge has been established, you will very soon progress to a more detailed study of the language of the play and the effects that it creates to bring the drama to life.

Here are some of the uses to which Shakespeare puts language:

- creating atmosphere
- in songs
- in dialogue
- in puns and wordplay.

Creating atmosphere

You should remember that in Shakespeare's time theatres did not have the elaborate scenery, backdrops and the sophisticated technology that is used to create effects in modern theatres. If you have ever visited Shakespeare's Globe in London or seen drawings of the Elizabethan theatre, you will know that they had little more than a bare stage. In that sense, theatregoers went to 'hear' a play rather than to 'see' a play as we would say today. The plays would also usually take place in daylight, without the elaborate lighting effects we are used to today.

Apart from all its other important functions, language was therefore essential to the creation of setting and atmosphere.

Songs

At first consideration, songs may not seem particularly important in the plays of Shakespeare, but it is interesting to note that twenty-six of his thirty-seven plays contain songs or parts of songs. Each of these is used quite deliberately to create a particular effect such as influencing the mood, giving us an insight into character, or echoing a theme.

Activity

Look at the play you are studying as part of your course. Does it have any songs in it? If it does, read them carefully and make notes on what they contribute to the play.

Dialogue

Dialogue is the means by which the characters communicate with each other, and it can take many different forms. Shakespeare uses short simple dialogue to create the impression of tension or rapid action; and he uses more intricate and poetic dialogue when presenting exchanges between lovers or the speeches of noble figures, like Kings, to their people. There are many ways in which dialogue might be structured to give a sense of atmosphere and tone in Shakespeare's drama. Look for features such as sentence length, rhythm and choice of vocabulory to help you analyse Shakespeare's dialogue effectively.

Activity

Look at the play you are studying and find three or four examples of contrasting uses of dialogue.

Puns and wordplay

Wordplay was much admired in Elizabethan England, and so it is no surprise that it is frequently used in the plays of Shakespeare. Puns were a particularly popular kind of wordplay. A pun is created when a word has two or more different meanings and the ambiguity is used to witty effect.

Activity

Look at the play you are studying and find some examples of wordplay. Explain what the wordplay consists of. What function does the wordplay serve in the context of the play?

Verse and prose

It has often been said that Shakespeare's greatness is rooted in his ability to use language to suit all moods, occasions, and characters. Much of his work is written in blank verse – a flexible form which he adapts to suit many purposes, from moments of intense passion, to bawdy bantering. However, Shakespeare also makes substantial use of prose, which prompts the question 'Why does he switch between verse and prose in his plays?'

A common answer to this question is that the 'high' characters use poetry, in keeping with their elevated natures and the substance of their dialogue, while the 'low' or comic characters use the more plebeian prose. An alternative interpretation is that Shakespeare uses prose for sub-plots, or to indicate madness or a highly-wrought emotional state in a character. It is easy to find examples to support these ideas, but examples can also be found to disprove them. The truth is that all these explanations are too general and simplistic to help us much, and the real explanation is rather more complex.

For example, *Hamlet* begins with the guards, Francisco and Barnardo, who are 'ordinary' and also, minor characters, speaking in verse. This helps to create a solemn and dignified tone with which to open the play, in keeping with the serious events that are about to unfold with the appearance of the Ghost. When Ophelia becomes mad she speaks prose but she also speaks prose in the 'play-within-the-play' scene where she is perfectly sane. Hamlet himself speaks both prose and verse depending on the situation and who he is speaking to. The Players speak prose when they are not performing and verse when they are in role.

In looking at Shakespeare's use of verse and prose, therefore, you need to look at the context of the specific episode to determine why Shakespeare has chosen to use language in the form he has. In every instance there will be a good dramatic reason on which his decision is based. Remember also that Shakespeare's prose is not an unplanned, casual form of writing. It is as much an art-form as his verse, and is just as carefully structured and organized.

Activity

Make a note of where switches between verse and prose occur in the text you are studying. Choose four examples. Give reasons why you think the switch is made in each case.

Critical works on Shakespeare

There have probably been more critical works written on Shakespeare than any other writer. This can give the impression that in order to understand his plays it is necessary to be familiar with the massive body of scholarship that attaches itself to his works. However, this is not the case.

When studying a Shakespeare play for AS or A2 Level, the first thing you should do is to try to make sense of it in your own terms. Reading the writings of literary critics can help to show the range of views that it is possible to take on almost any aspect of a Shakespeare play, but you must not let these views become substitutes for your own. Be aware that other views exist, and often can be well supported. Use them to help form your own ideas and sometimes to revise them, but do not be overawed by them. Words in print are not automatically 'true'. If you support your view with direct reference to the text, then you have a valid view.

2 Texts in context

Objectives

- to learn about various ways of placing texts in context
- to develop the ability to recognize and make use of relevant contextual information
- to prepare for studying and writing about the literature of a particular historical era or literary period

What do we mean by context?

When we study a poem, a play, a novel or any other piece of writing we may initially give our attention to exploring and analysing the text we see in front of us. However, no literary text can exist in a vacuum, or entirely on its own. All kinds of factors influence the way authors write and affect the way we read their work. Becoming aware of this background information can enhance our understanding and enjoyment of texts, by enabling us to see them as part of a wider picture. In other words, we place them in context.

There are several ways in which we can begin to place texts in context. We can consider:

- how a text interrelates with the events of the **author's life**
- the place of a particular text in the **author's *oeuvre*** or **writings as a whole**
- how the text reflects the **historical period** and/or the **place** in which it was written
- the text as an example of its **genre** or of a particular **literary style** or **period**
- the ways in which the **language** of a particular time or place is reflected in the text
- how our reading of the text might be influenced by the way other readers or critics have reacted to it recently or in the past – this is known as its **reception.**

Relevant contexts

At AS Level, at least part of your study of literature will be integrated with the study of a particular context – a historical era or literary period. This involves becoming familiar not only with the events, but also with the beliefs, ideas and concerns that have influenced or inspired the writers of that time. It works both ways, however. As you study the literary works, they themselves will reveal a lot about how society functioned at the time when they were written. You will be expected to recognize features that make a text typical – or atypical – of its context and to make your understanding clear by linking it with other texts you have read.

At A2 Level, you will study literature relating to a particular theme across the whole sweep of English Literature, from Chaucer to the present day. In doing so, you should develop an awareness of the differences between the literary styles and conventions of different times and contexts and learn how to draw comparisons between them. Here we will consider some methods of exploring literature from a contextual point of view.

The author's biography

It can certainly be interesting and increase our enjoyment of texts if we learn something about the lives of the people who wrote them. Indeed, it can be difficult to make any sense at all of some writing without any such knowledge. There can be two sides to this issue, however. Some critics believe that a text should stand alone and that as students of literature we should concern ourselves only with the words on the page; while others suggest that we should learn as much as possible about an author's life and times in order to understand the work fully. For AS and A2 Level, we are aiming to achieve a balance between these two approaches.

Some awareness of a writer's biography may be invaluable for understanding what lies behind the work, but it cannot take the place of thorough knowledge of the text itself and it can create some pitfalls. For example, in essays or exam answers, it may be tempting to include more of the writer's life story than necessary, if you have spent time learning about it. Unless you have specifically been asked to write about the text in this way, too much biographical information can waste valuable time and words that would be better spent focusing on the text itself. It is more important to demonstrate your understanding in more subtle ways, including facts or background details about the author only when they are clearly relevant to the points you want to make about the text.

Finding biographical information

As a starting point, editions intended for study, particularly of classics or older texts, often include an introduction with some biographical material. The best way to gain a deeper understanding of an author's life and times, however, is to read a good biography, or if one exists, an autobiography.

Biographies can vary enormously. Some can be thoroughly researched and packed with information but very dry and dull to read, while others may be enjoyable – even scandalous – but less accurate. It is worth dipping into a few, if they are available. It can be particularly interesting to compare the different viewpoints found in biographies written by contemporaries of the author with those written more recently. For example, *The Life of Charlotte Brontë* by Elizabeth Gaskell, published in 1857, gives not only a fascinating and personal account of her friend's life, but provides an inside view of society in the Victorian era. There are plenty of more recent biographies of the Brontës to read for a modern perspective.

You could also try the following:

- **Encyclopedias**
- **Diaries** or **letters** from the author, published in book form. These can give fascinating insights into a writer's life, and how and why he or she writes, as well as reflecting the events and concerns of the time.
- **Television documentaries** or **films** about the lives and times of famous writers.
- The **Internet**. Contemporary writers and associations of people interested in particular authors, such as The Brontë Society, often have websites, although you may have to search carefully for genuinely useful information.

The author's *oeuvre*

It can be important to know not only about the lives of writers but about their other works, so that you can see whether the text you are studying is typical of its author or whether it stands out for some reason. You may be asked to show that you are aware that authors can have favourite themes or features of style, which crop up regularly in their writings. For example, *The Handmaid's Tale* is typical of Margaret Atwood's work in that she frequently writes prose fiction about the roles and experiences of women in modern society. It is unusual, however, because it is the first novel in which she chooses to explore these ideas in a futuristic or science fiction setting.

Activity

1 Choose a writer whose work you are currently studying. Arrange for each member of your group to research one possible source of information about this author and make notes to bring to your next session. Aim to cover a range of sources, past and present, if that is relevant.

2 Discuss what you have discovered, noting any differences in your findings. Combine your information and create a handout on the life, work and times of your chosen writer.

Time and place

When you are studying texts in context, knowledge of the historical period and the location in which they were written is an essential tool for understanding the literature. Different times and places or cultures have conventions, styles or variations of language which, with experience, we can learn to recognize.

In this sense, place can be just as important as time. In recent decades there has been a surge of interest in the work of British writers who can trace their roots to other cultures, and in the literature of other English-speaking countries. Some of this is what we call post-colonial writing, by authors from nations which were previously colonies under the rule of European powers like the British Empire. Writers from the West Indies, India, and several African states, as well as from Canada and Australia, may fit this category. In a colony, the 'native' or indigenous culture may have been partly suppressed to make way for that which was imposed by the European invaders. With independence, there may be efforts to reassert the original culture. In any case, such societies are complex mixtures, often carrying the weight of the memory of oppression. The struggle to find a true sense of identity is a frequent theme.

If you are studying texts from this sort of background, find out as much as you can about the writer's cultural situation and the setting of the text. You should be aware that some of these writers use non-standard forms of the English language.

Literary period, style and genre

As well as relating texts to a historical period, we sometimes put them in the context of a **literary period** or style, which is not quite the same thing. Texts written around the same time are likely to have at least some similarities, but texts from a particular literary period are connected at a deeper level. Their authors are likely to share particular ideas about life, art and literature which are reflected in their work. They may be part of a 'movement' – a group of people who share a philosophy or belief system. Such groups tend to arise in response to political or social events, or out of a desire for change. For example, in the late eighteenth century, the Romantic movement was a reaction against the dry, formal, rather artificial styles of the previous decades. Writers embraced the spirit of revolution that was sweeping through Europe and America, and literature reflected a greater concern with nature, imagination and individual experience. A century or so later, in the years after the First World War, the Modernists experimented with artistic forms and styles. The old styles of art and writing no longer seemed appropriate in a world that had changed beyond recognition and which had ceased to make sense in the way it had done in the past.

When we talk about **literary genre,** we mean the particular kind or form of text we are reading: a play, novel, short story, biography or poem, for example. We might also focus on narrower categories, such as the Gothic novel, or Shakespearean tragedy.

Language

Language evolves continuously over time. We can see enormous differences between the language of our time and that of Chaucer or Shakespeare, but even in relatively recent texts, vocabulary and usage may be unfamiliar.

Language also alters with place. Within the British Isles, there are many varieties of English and quite a number of writers have experimented with these: from Emily Brontë's representation of Yorkshire dialect in *Wuthering Heights* to James Joyce's Irish English; or from Lewis Grassic Gibbon's Lowland Scots in *Sunset Song* to the broad Glaswegian of Irvine Welsh's *Trainspotting*. Also, as we have already mentioned, writers from other cultures may use forms of English other than Standard English. These are not 'wrong' or 'inferior', but are languages in their own right, with their own rules and structures.

Reception and critical context

As well as knowing something about the context in which a text is *written*, we also need to be aware that there is someone else in the equation: the *reader*. The background, culture or period in which we read a text may significantly influence how we react to it. Texts written in our own time, such as very recent novels, are difficult to categorize or place in context in quite the same way as we do with texts from the past, which have already been allocated to a period that has been given a name, like 'Romantic' or 'Victorian'. With older texts, we can also read the comments of critics, both those who wrote their responses when the text was first published and those who write with many years of hindsight; and all these ideas contribute something to our overall impression of the text. For example, it is interesting to learn that some of the first readers of Emily Brontë's famous novel *Wuthering Heights* called it respectively:

'The weirdest story in the English Language...'
'A nightmare.'
'A world of brilliant figures in an atmosphere of mist...'
'One of the most repellent books we ever read.'
'[A book that] shows more genius... than you will find in a thousand novels.'

Critics and readers ever since have continued to respond to the novel in different ways, depending on their own backgrounds and ideas.

If you go on to study literature at a higher level, you will have more exposure to the writings of literary critics and also to various literary **theories**. The ideas and approaches that these offer can be useful in stimulating new ways of looking at texts and can often prompt ideas that might not have occurred to you had you not read them. It does not matter whether you agree or disagree with the ideas you read. Challenging the things that you read by giving your own evidence in support of an alternative view, is always much more effective than quietly agreeing with everything you read.

Literary theory

Many of the critics you will read will approach their analysis of the text using a particular theory that they apply to all texts. There are many of these literary theories, most of which have been developed by academics over the past three or four decades, sometimes running counter to one another. The main thing to remember is that each one looks at a text from a particular point of view, or focuses on a certain aspect of it. This is because the theory regards one particular aspect of the text as being more significant than anything else. It is important to keep this in mind when reading literary analysis based on individual literary theories. The following are brief descriptions of the more important literary theories. You may well have already come across some of these. (Bear in mind, though, that these descriptions only give you a very simple definition of very complex theories.)

Structuralism

This is a complex theory, but essentially it involves the reader giving up his or her right to a personal response and focusing on the text alone to describe how the text operates. The theory involves taking a much more 'scientific' approach, with the belief that all texts attempt to create a view of the world by ordering it through the structure of language. The effect of a structuralist approach can be to look closely at the language structures of a text and to place less emphasis on what a text tells us about life, the world and the characteristics of human nature. The latter are more common approaches at A Level.

Post-structuralism or deconstructive criticism

Post-structuralism covers a whole range of activities, so again the ideas are very much simplified here. Post-structuralism questions the structuralist idea that the reader must have knowledge of the literary code of language in order to gain access to the meaning of a text. It does not regard the meaning in language as being stable. It also argues that the reader's perceptions of a text are necessarily subjective so that the idea of any kind of literary objectivity is brought into question. As post-structuralist criticism seeks to destabilize the text by demonstrating its contradictions and problems, it has sometimes been regarded as quite a destructive form of criticism. However it can also have more positive effects. For example, it can encourage you to consider alternative meanings and see the text as dynamic, rather than something that has closed meanings.

Psychoanalytical theory

Psychoanalytical theory has made a major contribution to post-structuralist theory, by taking as its starting point the ideas of Sigmund Freud, who sought to provide by universal models and explanations for the unconscious drives that motivate human behaviour. Jacques Lacan developed Freud's theories further through his view that language is the major force in shaping human identity. These theories have been applied to literature study and can provide new angles on the ways in which texts are constructed and presented.

Marxist criticism

Unlike structuralist and post-structuralist literary theories, which have nothing to do with history, society and class in relation to a text, the Marxist critic brings to a text Karl Marx's view of history in which the idea of class struggle is central. It promotes analysis of a text by creating connections between the text itself and the social and economic structure of the society in which it was written. The theory regards these connections as being fundamental to the nature of the literature produced. Marxist criticism challenges many of the traditional views of texts which interpret them according to the values of a bourgeois or middle-class culture. It seeks to move away from the idea that texts present universal truths about human nature, looking instead to reinterpret a text in light of the period in which it was written and the nature of the society that influenced it.

Feminist criticism

Like Marxist criticism, feminist criticism also concerns itself with social and political issues, in this case with the presentation of women in literature. The feminist critic is particularly interested in seeking to affirm feminine qualities within what is regarded as a male-dominated society. Most feminist criticism takes as its starting point the idea that society is and always has been patriarchal (male-dominated) and examines texts from this perspective.

An important element within feminist criticism is that of black, women-of-colour, and lesbian critical theory. Writers and critics involved in this area are concerned with the interrelationship between race, sexuality and oppression.

An overview

This very brief look at some of the key critical theories, shows just a few examples of the varying ways in which texts can be considered. Your understanding of such theories can contribute to your overall understanding of literature, but you should always be aware that they all approach the analysis of texts from a very particular, even partisan, point of view.

As you take your studies further, your awareness and sensitivity to the layers of meaning within literary texts will continue to grow, but never forget that the fundamental element in this process is to develop your own view. Your view of a text is as valid as anyone else's, so long as it is based firmly on a study of the text itself – it is vital that your view incorporates 'creative, informed, and relevant responses' to the text.

3 Writing about texts

Objectives

- to suggest a range of ways to read and make notes in preparation for writing
- to introduce different strategies for planning writing
- to study the effective use of quotation in essays
- to consider the features of clear structure in literary essays
- to identify formal and objective elements of style and develop a personal style of writing

Planning strategies

Whether you are writing an essay for classwork, in an exam, or beginning a major piece of coursework, it can often be difficult to get started. However, there are several measures you can take to make this easier. There are also ways of thinking and planning beforehand that can help you feel more confident and secure about essay writing.

Many students find it best to develop their own preparing and planning methods, which can be used in exams as well as for less formal pieces of writing. However, it is a good idea to try out several different methods and then choose those that work best for you. Your choice will depend on your learning style. For example, some people naturally find it easier to grasp information when it is presented using pictures and diagrams, while others are more comfortable with words, and prefer information written in list or note form. Experiment to find which ones are most helpful to you.

Analyzing the question

After studying the text or passage, consider the question you plan to answer very carefully. Check that you understand it fully. What are its key words and ideas? Underline them, like this:

Either

'Iago "rewrites" *Othello*: a play which begins as a romantic comedy, but which ends as a tragedy.'

Evaluate the relationship between tragedy and comedy in *Othello* in the light of this comment.

Or

Othello has been described as 'fatally self-centred' and 'lacking in self knowledge'.

Evaluate Shakespeare's presentation of Othello in the light of this view.

The underlined words represent the ideas that you will need to keep in mind while you plan and write your answer. In addition to identifying these specific points, do not forget that the hidden message in all questions is that you should write about *how* the writer has used language to create effects.

Annotating the text

When you are preparing to write an essay, annotating your text can be very useful. It can help you to remember certain details and enable you to find them again during revision. This is especially true when you are working with a long text. It is also true whether the text is a complete novel or a play you are studying for coursework, or your wider reading.

Remember that both of your exams will be closed book exams, which means you will not be able to take a copies of the texts in with you. Annotating for revision however, is still very useful, and if the texts you are using in class cannot be annotated then you may like to buy a copy of your own to use for this purpose.

If you already have an essay question or a topic to focus on when you read and annotate, it will be easier to recognize the relevant information, lines and phrases from the text for you to underline or highlight.

Colour coding

One additional useful way of annotating, which will keep your text uncluttered and help you to find the parts that you want quickly, is to use a system of colour coding. Using this system you can underline or sideline references relating to different themes, topics and characters in different colours. As long as you know what the colour signifies and you do not overdo it, it can really help you to find your way around the text quickly. This is useful whether you are preparing for an essay or revising for an exam.

Making notes

There are many different ways of writing or organizing your notes on a text. Here are some to try:

Listing key points

Quickly make a list of four to six points which you would need to cover in order to answer the different aspects of the question. Try to arrange them in a logical order, so that you can move easily from one to another as you write. Often, it is best to begin with the most general point and then move on to more specific points. If you are answering an exam question, four to six points should be sufficient.
(If you are writing a larger-scale essay for coursework, you will probably need a longer list.) An answer which included a paragraph on each point on your list would cover the main points appropriate to the essay question.

Using diagrams

Try writing your key words or topic headings in the middle of a blank sheet of paper. Write words or phrases for related ideas around them, working outwards towards more detailed points. Link the words in as many ways as possible and circle or highlight ideas of most importance. Some people who use these say that you can begin your essay with any point on your diagram and find a way to work through all your ideas. Others prefer to start from one of the topic headings.

Charting information

Devise your own ways of arranging information in diagram form. For example, family trees can help sort out complex relationships, or you could use a graph to plot the ups and downs of a character's life. If the essay question asks you to consider two sides argumentatively, or involves a comparison, then listing the opposing ideas in a table can also help.

Arranging ideas on cards

Write important points and related quotations, or notes for the individual paragraphs you want to include, on cards. You can then arrange these, like jigsaw pieces, in different ways until you work out the best order in which to write about them.

This technique is not suitable for exam situations! It is most useful when you are working on a long text and need to collect notes and examples on a theme or character as you read.

Finding your own strategies

Activity

Having seen the various strategies in action in this unit, try out at least three using an extract from one of your set texts.

As you work on each technique, decide how successful it is for you and which methods you find most fruitful in your interpretation of the text.

We do need to remember, however, that sometimes the process of writing is in itself an exploration. At times we need to throw away all our plans and plunge into the writing before we can find out exactly what our ideas are; some arguments and ideas only take shape when we have worked through them in writing. Some writers always work this way and are not comfortable with planning in advance.

The most important thing is that you discover planning strategies that work for you, and use them so that they become a natural part of your writing process. Then you will have a familiar starting point when faced with the pressure of exam conditions.

Using evidence from the text effectively

Once you have done some planning for the question you will be writing about, you will have established the main points that you want to convey in your essay and perhaps even feel that you have an answer. However, as you write, it is essential that you provide some good reasons and evidence to support what you say. Evidence in this sense means examples and quotations from the text.

It is not very useful, for example, to write that a poet 'uses a great deal of alliteration' in a poem. That would be to make an assertion without giving any grounds for it. All it would demonstrate is that you can recognize alliteration and that you know the technical term for it. You need to follow this statement with some quotations from the poem which contain alliteration. From there you will need to go on and *analyse* the quotation and comment on the *effect* created by the alliteration. So, broadly speaking, the process of literary comment has three stages.

> **Three steps to using evidence effectively**
>
> **1** State the point you wish to make.
>
> **2** Follow this with your quotation, making sure the context of the quotation is clear, by briefly explaining the situation, or who is speaking and to whom. Quotations should be presented in speech marks or clearly differentiated from the rest of your writing.
>
> **3** Analyse the quotation in detail, commenting on individual words or phrases and explaining how and why they are used and with what effect.

Of course, you will not want to keep rigidly to this three-stage process of statement, quotation, analysis as; that would produce rather mechanical essays. However, it is useful to bear these three steps in mind until it becomes integrated into your writing. Two of the most common difficulties students have with essay-writing arise from the use of quotations:

- **Context:** not providing enough information to make sense of quotations. In other words, sprinkling quotations throughout essays without providing crucial details about what is going on in the text or which character is speaking. Do not fall into the trap however, of spending all your time paraphrasing the text; It is a fine balance to achieve.

- **Analysis:** students usually find this third stage of the process the most challenging. However, its importance is shown in the A Level marking criteria, where the ability to be analytical gains candidates higher grades.

You will no doubt find your study of literature more rewarding when you know how to recognize and comment on the important details of how writers use language. It will also help you to become more aware of the language choices you make when you are writing yourself.

Structuring an essay

There is no one structure that will work for every essay. Each question will demand a slightly different approach, as the following guidelines illustrate. Here is a basic essay framework:

1 Introduction

Briefly outline the subject of the essay; it can be useful to refer to the question and its key words and ideas.

Sometimes in coursework it can be useful to give a very concise introduction to the text(s) you are writing about. This might include one or two sentences to establish the context of the question, for example, in terms of plot or character. It is vital that you do not tell the story at length. All your time and effort should be devoted to answering the question.

2 Main section

This could take several different forms, depending on the type of question that you are answering.

- If the question has several key words or ideas, or asks you to explore more than one aspect of the text, you may be able to see a ready-made structure for the main part of your essay.

- If you have already thought about the question and made a plan, you can then set about working through the topics in your list or diagram, presenting them in an order which allows you to move easily from one to another.

- If the question requires you to consider two sides of an argument before concluding with your own views, you can organize your writing in one of two ways:

  either

  Present all the arguments on one side first, making sure you always support your ideas with evidence. Then repeat the process for the other side of the argument.

  or

  Make a table showing the arguments on each side of the question, then work through them in a 'zig-zag' fashion, presenting an argument from one side followed by an argument from the other side, and so on until you have covered all the points you wish to make. This may seem harder to do, but can often have more impact.

3 Conclusion

Once you have explored all the ideas or arguments you want to mention, finish by explaining the conclusion you have reached and/or briefly summing up the most important points you have made. Sometimes it is useful to restate the key words and ideas from the question in your conclusion. Try to express your conclusion clearly. An otherwise good essay can be marred by a weak ending, and you want to leave your reader with a good impression!

Maintaining an argument

Whatever type of essay you are working on, it is always essential to keep the central issue(s) of the question in mind. After each point or idea you discuss, check that you have made clear how it relates to your overall argument.

If you have recently studied a GCSE English course, you will probably have learned how to make use of the 'argument marker' words and phrases, which are an invaluable aid to structuring arguments. As long as you don't use them too mechanically, they can help to guide the reader through your ideas and make your writing flow.

Adding more sophistication

The above essay structure is quite straightforward. You will often find, however, that in following a line of argument, it is necessary to explore a side issue or a related topic before returning to your central theme. It is vital that you can do this without becoming sidetracked and never returning to the main path, or jumping jarringly from one idea to another.

Activity

1 Swap one of your recent essays for one by a partner. Assess your partner's essay. In particular, look at the structure of the essay and how evidence from the text has been used.

- Annotate it to show where the structure is clear and informative and where this could be improved.

- Comment on where quotations have been used effectively and where they are less successful.

2 Hand back the annotated essays and discuss the comments you have made with your partner.

Getting tone and style right

Until you are familiar with the conventions for writing literary criticism, it may be difficult to grasp exactly what kind of tone or style is appropriate for writing your essays. One way to approach this is to read some good critical writing to get the 'feel' of it. Collections of critical writing which contain essays and reviews relating to a particular author, or to specific texts, can be useful in this respect. These often illustrate widely differing points of view and so serve as good reminders that there is rarely only one way to interpret a text. As well as introducing you to some different ways of thinking about the texts you are studying, they will help you to develop your awareness of the accepted language of criticism.

In studying A Level Literature, there should be opportunities for you to express your own responses to texts as well as writing objectively about them. However, the more objective approach always needs to form the backbone of your critical writing, and when you do express your opinions or feelings about the effectiveness of a piece of writing, you need to support them with reasoned evidence. Usually this evidence will take the form of quotations from the text. Beware of writing statements like 'The imagery in stanza two is extremely evocative and effective' or 'I found this chapter very moving' – and leaving it at that. You need to provide specific examples or quotations and explain how the lines are effective, and why.

Examiners will always look for well-supported ideas and interpretations that you have worked out for yourself. They may also look for your understanding of other people's readings of the text, particularly if you are writing about a text in terms of its historical or critical context. When you include the views of other critics, these need to be presented as quotations and acknowledged. Otherwise you run the risk of plagiarizing: 'borrowing', or even stealing, someone else's ideas and presenting them as your own. You will be severely penalized if you do this in exams or coursework.

Formality of style

In order to write successfully you will need to adopt an appropriate formality style. This can be difficult to define, but there are some points to note.

Things to avoid are the following:

- **The first person:** Generally, avoid *over-using* the first person in your responses. For example, rather than saying 'I think Louisa is imaginative because…', try to use expressions like 'Dickens suggests that Louisa has a vivid imagination by…' or 'It appears that Louisa is imaginative because…'. Having said that, the occasional use of 'I' or 'me' in a piece of critical commentary to reinforce an important point or to express a personal response can be most effective.

- **Slang:** Avoid using slang expressions (unless, of course, they appear in quotations from your text!). Colloquial language is the language of informal speech. Try to develop your awareness of the differences between spoken English and written English.

- **Dialect and local usage:** Some words or expressions may be used only in some parts of the country; these are appropriate in some forms of writing, but in a formal essay, Standard English is preferable.

- **Abbreviations:** It is better not to use abbreviated forms in formal writing. For example, write 'did not' rather than 'didn't'; and avoid using 'etc.'.

- **Numbers:** These should be written in word form, for example, 'thirty-seven' rather than '37', unless the figure is very large.

However, **do** use:

- **The present tense:** Most literary criticism is written in the present tense. This is because the text itself, whether a novel or a poem, always exists in the same way, even though the narrative may be in the past tense. Aim to keep your writing in the present tense. For example, 'The opening scenes of the play take place in…' not '… took place in …'. It is even more important to be consistent: whether you use present or past tense, make sure you use the same one throughout. There are many examples of critical responses written in the present tense throughout this book.

The craft in your writing

As your study of literature progresses, you will develop an awareness of the variety of ways in which writers use language. You may begin to think of writing as a craft: something which most writers think about and work at with great care and attention to detail, rather than something which simply happens haphazardly.

Try to think about your own writing in the same way.

- Make deliberate choices about the vocabulary you use, choosing the best word for the job, rather than the first one that comes to mind.

- Try out different lengths and types of sentences.
- Think about the contrasting ideas you wish to include in your paragraphs.
- Try to weigh ideas against each other when you are writing argumentatively.

Activity

Re-read some of your own recent essays. What are the strengths and weaknesses of your written style? Think about this carefully yourself and ask a teacher for feedback. Choose one weakness (for example, not putting quotations properly in context or failing to comment on them in detail; inconsistent use of tenses; poor punctuation) and focus on correcting this in your next essay.

Some fortunate people – usually those who have read very widely – seem to have an innate sense of how to write appropriately for different purposes. Others only develop a sense of style with practice. The aim is to reach the point where you know you can communicate ideas clearly and that you are in complete control of your writing.

4 AS coursework

Objectives

- to think about requirements for your written AS coursework
- to consider the kinds of tasks you will need to undertake
- to think about the use of secondary sources and writing a bibliography
- to develop the ability to explore relationships and comparisons between literary texts

What are the benefits of coursework?

The benefits that the coursework element can bring to a course and the breadth that it can give to your studies are well acknowledged.

In particular coursework can:

- offer you freedom in terms of choice of texts and more of a say in the nature of the work you undertake
- provide you with opportunities to set your own tasks and pursue particular literary interests, so developing more independence in your learning
- allow you to produce work free of the constraints of exam conditions so that you can present more carefully planned and considered responses, through using the drafting process
- develop skills which will help you perform more effectively in the exams
- help you to gain experience in undertaking research and wider reading in preparation for studying English at degree level.

Coursework folder requirements

For your AS coursework you will study three post-1900 texts, one of which must have been first published or performed after 1990. At least two of the texts must be literary, but can be any combination of poetry, prose and drama. One literary text may be a text in translation, if it can be considered significant or influential. One text may be a work of literary criticism or cultural commentary. None of the texts chosen should appear on the set text lists for AS or A2. The coursework task will present you with opportunities to understand and appreciate literary texts in light of other readers' views and to draw connections between texts.

You will need to complete **two** pieces of writing. The maximum word limit **including** both pieces is **3000 words**.

Piece 1

You have a choice as to the kind of task you write. It can be **either**:

a) A critical analysis. You should select a small section of text: of up to **three pages** of prose or drama, or **forty lines** of poetry, and write a close analysis of it.

b) An item of re-creative writing based on a selected passage. You will also need to write a commentary explaining the link between your writing and the original passage selected.

You will need to include a copy of your chosen passage in your coursework folder. **This task must be based on a single literary text**.

Piece 2

The second piece of writing in your folder will be an essay comparing and contrasting two texts, informed by other readers' interpretations. The term 'other readers' includes any of the following:

- the opinions of recognized critics
- different theatrical performances
- concepts such as the Aristotelian concept of tragedy
- theories such as Marxist or feminist approaches to texts
- different adaptations such as film or television versions of texts.

The texts chosen should be grouped to allow scope for links and contrasts between them.

The following are some examples of the kinds of tasks that might be suitable:

- Texts exploring the theme of innocence to experience: *'Rites of passage or baptisms of fire are part of the process of growing up.' Compare and contrast the ways in which two of your chosen writers present growing up in light of this comment.*

- Adventure or fantasy texts: *'Narrative method drives all fantasy fiction.' Compare and contrast ways in which features of narrative method such as voice, style and structure drive two of your chosen adventure/fantasy texts.*

- Texts exploring the theme of belief systems in the modern world: *'Religion is both a cohesive and divisive social force.' Compare ways in which two of your writers present the influence religion has on society.*

Assessment Objectives

Your work for this unit will be assessed against the following Assessment Objectives. The first piece of work will be assessed against AO1 and AO2, and the second against AO1, AO3 and AO4.

AO1 Articulate creative, informed and relevant responses to literary texts, using appropriate terminology and concepts, and coherent, accurate written expression.

AO2 Demonstrate detailed critical understanding in analysing the ways in which structure, form and language shape meaning in literary texts.

AO3 Explore connections and comparisons between different literary texts, informed by interpretations of other readers.

AO4 Demonstrate understanding of the significance and influence of the contexts in which literary texts are written and received.

Suggested word counts

Your complete AS coursework folder must not run over **3000 words**. If you do go beyond this limit then only the first 3000 words of your work will be marked. Although you are free to divide the word limit how you wish between tasks, it is a good idea to look closely at the marks available for each question and use this as guidance as to the relative lengths of the pieces within your coursework folder.

Task 1, which includes the close reading or re-creative piece, is worth **15 marks**, whilst Task 2, the essay on linked texts is worth **25 marks**. With this in mind, it would be wise to set aside approximately 1000–1200 words for Task 1, reserving at least 1800–2000 words for Task 2. The word counts are something that you should bear in mind from the outset of the unit so that you can plan your coursework effectively.

Writing the commentary

If you choose to carry out the re-creative task with the commentary for Task 1 then you will also have to determine how to divide the 1000–1200 words that you have dedicated to this task between two separate pieces of work.

When attempting to decide upon this, it is important to understand that the re-creative writing piece is not, in itself, enough to qualify for many of the marks available. The task is marked in a way that requires you to provide evidence of skills in both the re-creative piece and the commentary, and some marks are reserved entirely for the commentary.

In order to get good marks for Task 1, you will have to make accurate use of critical terminology in the commentary. You will also have to present a structured and detailed argument, demonstrate effective analytical methods and make good use of quotations and references, blending them into your writing. It is not possible to successfully demonstrate any of these abilities in Task 1 if you do not produce a well-considered and developed commentary alongside your re-creative piece of writing.

In many respects, factors such as the originality, artistic merit and length of the re-creative piece are of much lower importance than showing an excellent understanding of the original text and supporting this with a technically accurate, well-structured and perceptive commentary.

Making connections

We make connections and comparisons between experiences every day and the study of literature provides you with the opportunity to practice this skill more consciously in relation to the texts you study. Learning to compare related literary texts to each other by linking their themes, or by analysing how authors can deal with the same topic in radically different ways, can be both fascinating and satisfying.

To make an effective comparison between your texts, you will need to study them in detail first. Once you know them well, you can then begin to organize your ideas from a comparative perspective. In order to keep track of your ideas about two (or more) texts, you may find it helpful to use a diagram or table to organize them before you start to write. Sometimes, you will find that the contrasts between texts become more apparent once you have made the connections; that the differences grow out of the similarities. This is one possible way of organizing your ideas.

Here is an example, using a pair of novels which share a theme: *The Color Purple* by Alice Walker and *Oranges Are Not the Only Fruit* by Jeanette Winterson.

A woman's struggle: *The Color Purple/Oranges Are Not the Only Fruit*

Connections		Contrasts
Both novels trace a girl's struggle to grow up and achieve independence in a hostile, prejudiced or limiting environment.	But	They are set in very different environments and contexts. Celie in *The Color Purple* grows up as a black woman in the Deep South of America in the 1930s facing the oppression not just of her sex but of her race. Jeanette, in Lancashire, England, in the 1960s has to contend with the overpowering domination of her mother and the narrow-minded beliefs of the religious group in which she is brought up.
Both novels explore feminist themes and feature strong female characters (Jeanette's mother/Sofia). Jeanette and Celie both have female 'mentors' or role models who encourage them to find their own inner strength (Elsie/ Shug Avery).	But	Sofia and Shug are sympathetic characters who are powerful and assert their own rights, while Jeanette's mother is oppressive as well as impressive.
Male characters are weak.	But	They show it in different ways. Jeanette's father is hardly there at all – he simply opts out of asserting himself. Men like 'Mr___' and Harpo hide their feelings of impotence behind violence and vindictiveness – usually against women. The men in *Oranges Are Not the Only Fruit* do not develop, but in *The Color Purple*, men learn something too.
Celie and Jeanette are both empowered by lesbian relationships.	But	Celie's relationship with Shug is life-enhancing and leads through to greater acceptance of herself and an ability to relate on an equal basis with both men and women. Jeanette discovers her sexuality, an important part of her identity, through her relationship with Melanie, but has to cope with betrayal and denunciation before going on alone to find her own way as a lesbian.
Both challenge the traditional forms of the Christian religion which have restricted their freedom to grow.	But	In Celie's case this means ridding herself of the image of a white, male, judgemental God and replacing it with a more inclusive loving presence, while Jeanette concludes by questioning the existence of God altogether.

| Both are narrated in the first person and use some unconventional narrative techniques. | **But** | Most of *Oranges Are Not the Only Fruit* is presented as a fairly traditional, past-tense narrative; this is interrupted by reflective passages and fairy tales or fables, told in the third person, which run parallel or act as a commentary. *The Color Purple* is constructed as a series of letters, a device that makes possible the immediacy of the present tense. |
| Both writers challenge us with their use of language. | **But** | Winterson uses a great deal of religious and Biblical vocabulary and allusion. Without knowledge of this, some of her ideas and humour will be lost on us. *The Color Purple* is not 'difficult' in this way, but is written in a form of Black American English that may be unfamiliar to some readers. |

Writing a comparative essay

When you come to structure your essay for Task 2 of Unit F662, there are a number of approaches available. Two methods that we will look at here are the anchor method and the integrated method.

Whichever of the methods you choose, you must remember that it would be virtually impossible to cover all possible elements of similarity and contrast. You should concentrate on selecting an appropriate focus for your comparative essay and ensuring that you develop an opinion or argument that will drive your essay forward. This argument will need to be developed by first choosing a focus for your comparison and secondly by providing evidence from your texts to support your particular point of view.

The anchor text method

To apply this method, you should start by analysing one text, and then compare parts of the other text to it: this is called *using an anchor text*. Try to use one text as the starting point of your analysis and then compare the other text or texts to it. When you do this, you must ensure that you approach the first text with a particular focus, to allow you to bring in the comparative analysis of the other texts in a logical and constructive way.

The risk with this method is that you are tempted to write about the texts separately and that your work subsequently fails to demonstrate your abilities to link and compare the texts. The advantage of this method is that you can decide which text to start with, often the most substantial or the one that you think is the most accessible to you, and then decide how you will link the other text or texts to this discussion. The disadvantage, of course, is that some sections of your essay, where you focus on your anchor text will not be comparative. For this reason, it is important that you provide a close comparison when you bring the other text or texts into your essay.

This is an outline of the way you might approach your essay, if you use this method:

* choose which text you are going to start with
* plan what you are going to say about it
* use your plan on the first text to help you find comparisons with the other text or texts

- write about your anchor text first
- pick out relevant comparisons which help you to show meaningful differences between the texts
- supplement evidence from your texts with ideas and insights that you have gained from considering other readers
- use key comparative words to help you, for instance: *however, but, in comparison to, though, similarly*
- use critical terminology to clarify your points of comparison
- use ideas about the context of each text to develop the comparative points that you make, keeping all references to context tightly focused and closely tied to the text
- remember to use the three-point critical sentences throughout; ensuring they each consist of a point, followed by evidence from the text and an explanation.

The integrated method

The difference between this method and the anchor text method is that you compare your texts *from the outset*. This means that you can choose the focus that you feel will benefit your answer most. It is, however, still necessary to use a structure to build your answer around. Here is one way of approaching your integrated comparison:

- decide upon the ways you can compare the texts
- use a logical order
- make reference to what you know about the context of each text to help explain and illuminate your comparative points
- use key comparative words to help you, for instance: *however, but, in comparison to, though, similarly*
- supplement your own views with what you have discovered through looking at the opinions of other readers
- remember to use the three-point critical sentence throughout
- use technical vocabulary to help explain comparative points clearly.

Potential problem areas

Overall, examiners report that a high standard of work is produced by students through coursework. However, here are some points that they have highlighted as weaknesses or problem areas in some of the work they have assessed:

- inappropriately framed or worded assignments
- tasks that focus on a general discussion of themes or 'character studies': these tend to lack interest and focus
- questions that do not require close attention to the text and critical judgement
- the inclusion of too much biographical or historical background
- too much narrative retelling of the plot or events.

It is important that your question is carefully constructed to allow you to meet the Assessment Objectives against which it will be judged. Your teacher has an important role to play in helping you frame your question in the right way and you must ensure that your response addresses the issues discussed here.

The use of secondary sources

It is essential for this unit that you use secondary sources to help you formulate your response. In producing coursework, it is also important that you learn how to refer to and acknowledge these sources correctly. Clearly, the primary source for your work is the text that you are studying. The secondary sources are any other materials that help you in your work, such as study aids, critical books, or articles about the text. It can also be useful to 'read around the text' – to learn about the history, the art, and the music of the time in which it was written.

Whilst using secondary sources can certainly help to broaden your view of the text and show you other ways of looking at it, remember that there are rarely right answers as far as literature is concerned. All texts are open to a variety of interpretations: your view can be informed by other sources, but never let these views substitute your own. Have confidence in your views, develop your own voice, and avoid plagiarism (even accidental) at all costs. This means that where you use secondary source material you must make sure that you acknowledge every text and list it in the bibliography at the end of your assignment.

It is also worth noting at this point that for both this unit and unit F664, quotations, footnotes and bibliographies **do not** count towards the 3000 word limit.

Bibliography

In order to acknowledge appropriately the books and other materials that you have read or consulted while writing your coursework essay, it is important to understand the conventions of bibliography writing. Even if you have read only a part of a particular book or article it should be included in your bibliography.

Your bibliography should be arranged in the following format:

- surname of the author (authors listed alphabetically)
- initials of the author
- title of the book (italics or underlined) or article (inverted commas) and source
- publisher's name
- date of publication (usually the date when first published).

Here is an example of how a bibliography might look, taking into account all the above points:

Bibliography

Chilcott, T., *A Critical Study of the Poetry of John Clare*, Hull University Press, 1985

Drabble, M. (ed.) *The Oxford Companion to English Literature*, Oxford University Press, 1985

Ford, B. (ed.) *Victorian Britain*, Cambridge University Press, 1989

Gibson, J. and Johnson, T. (eds.), *Thomas Hardy Poems: A Casebook*, Macmillan, 1979

Johnson, T., *A Critical Introduction to the Poems of Thomas Hardy*, St Martin's Press, 1991

Activity

Using your library or learning resource centre, find at least five books or articles on a particular topic, text or author. Find the information that you would need for a bibliography, such as the author, publisher, and publication date and then, using the examples above as a guide, place them in the correct order, as though you were creating a bibliography for a piece of coursework.

5 The extended essay

Objectives

- to prepare for the task of writing an extended essay, and successfully complete the various steps needed in the process
- to build the ability to work independently and make informed choices of texts, topics and questions
- to further develop the skill of exploring relationships and comparisons between literary texts

Working on an extended essay for coursework offers you an opportunity to work independently and to develop skills that will be very useful if you go on to study literature or other arts subjects at a higher level. You may have the opportunity to select some of the texts that you study and to devise your own question or theme to explore. This may seem daunting at first, but your teachers or lecturers will offer help and support. Most students gain a sense of great satisfaction and 'ownership' from completing an extended essay. It can help you to develop confidence in your own ideas, which is invaluable if you plan to study at university, where you will be expected to organize your own work and think independently.

The extended essay requires you to undertake the comparison of three texts of your own choice, linked, for example, by movement, time of writing, form, values, gender or theme. The texts must include one prose and one poetry text; the third text can be from any genre. All three texts can be selected from any period and from across periods. Your essay should have a maximum of **3000 words**.

Making connections

Learning to relate literary texts to each other by linking their themes, or by considering how the situations they present can appear to be very different and yet be parallel, or by analysing how authors can deal with the same topic in radically different ways, can be fascinating.

For Advanced Level courses, particularly at A2 Level, you will be expected to demonstrate that you can recognize and understand literary connections like these and explore them effectively in writing. There are several situations in which your ability to compare texts will be assessed, but in the extended essay, it will be your chief concern.

Prepare to compare

Writing comparatively about multiple texts is inevitably a more complex process that writing about a single one. Sometimes, particularly when under pressure, it may seem easier to resort to writing first about one text and then about the other. However, this is not true comparative writing and rarely produces a satisfactory result. It is much better to develop the skill of weaving together your ideas about all of the texts throughout your writing, even if this seems more difficult initially. There are some strategies you can use when preparing to write comparatively, which may help to make this easier.

In order to compare full-length texts for your extended essay, you will need to know them well enough to select appropriate material as required and to be comfortable moving backwards and forwards from one to the other. Once you have studied each text, find ways of organizing your thoughts and ideas effectively, not just about one text at a time but by dealing with them together.

When preparing to undertake your extended essay, you will need to gather information before making a series of choices. The suggestions offered here are intended to help you in situations where you are working on a topic of your own choice, with the support of a teacher or supervisor. The tasks you should complete can be broken down into the following stages:

Preparation

1 Choosing suitable texts – this may be done with your teacher or lecturer
2 Getting to know your material
3 Clarifying your ideas
4 Formulating a question
5 Research and note-taking

Following this you will need to plan your response to your chosen question and begin writing. This task can also be broken down into various stages:

Writing

1 Planning
2 Writing a draft
3 Revising and editing
4 The final version
5 Presenting your work

1 Choose your texts

The first step in the process is to choose the texts that you are going to study and write about. Some teachers and lecturers may help you to choose your texts but you need to bear in mind that the texts you use should be 'literary' and of sufficient quality to justify the effort you will put into studying them. However, because you are likely to be working on your extended essay over a period of several months, and will need to get to know your chosen books very well, it is also important that you choose texts that you enjoy and find interesting or inspiring in some way. You are likely to enjoy the task and produce a much more successful essay if you are studying a subject that is personally meaningful to you.

Above all, the texts should have some clear connections that will enable you to write an effective comparative study. They should not only give you the chance to discuss interesting links and parallels in plot, characters and theme, but should also provide you with opportunities to explore and comment on:

- the writers' styles and techniques
- choices of genre
- different narrative techniques
- individual choices of language and their effects
- the different ways writers structure ideas and develop similar themes.

You may already have some ideas about texts that interest you, but here are some suggestions to aid the process:

- Use one of the Shakespeare plays you have studied as a starting point. Map out or list the themes that are highlighted in the play. For example, *Romeo & Juliet* is about tragic love, love and conflict, forbidden love, love between people from divided backgrounds; *King Lear* involves themes of youth versus old age, madness, conflict between parents and children, misconceptions of reality, loyalty; *Othello* includes mixed-race marriage, jealousy and deceit. Choose one of these themes and look for texts by other writers who have explored it in their work in similar or contrasting ways.
- Teachers may set up a special session or meeting where there will be lots of texts available for you to browse through and a chance to discuss your ideas and interests individually. They can help to suggest texts that will interest you and point out possible connections between them.
- You may have read a book that you particularly enjoyed and want to use in your essay, but need some help with choosing other texts. Think about what made the book interesting to you and ask your teachers for suggestions.
- Do some research on your own. If your school or college has a library, set aside some time to explore the books that are available. Browsing in public libraries and bookshops can be useful too.
- Ask around. Friends, family and fellow students may be able to recommend books they have enjoyed.

2 Get to know your material

Once you have become familiar with your texts, you should be able to find material as you need it and to be comfortable moving backwards and forwards from one to the other.

- Start by reading each of your texts straight through to gain an overview – and for enjoyment. If you have already studied the Shakespeare play, watch a film version of it or try to see a live performance. You will already have ideas about some of the connections between your texts, or themes you plan to write about, so keep these in the back of your mind as you read.
- Do some research about the contexts of your texts. When were they written? What was going on at the time? How may this have influenced the authors?
- Once you know your way around the texts and their main themes, you will also wish to read some critical material and interpretations of your texts. This can help you see the texts in different ways and spark ideas for essay questions, but remember that other peoples' views are only a part of the exercise and can never be a substitute for your own considered opinions, based on your careful reading of the texts.

3 Clarify your ideas

Once you have a good overview of each text, you need to find ways of focusing your thoughts and ideas effectively, not just about one text at a time but about all the texts together. This will help you in the process of formulating connections and contrasts.

It is usually helpful to focus first on the **connections**. Establish the major links between the texts first, making sure that you are clear about any similarities in themes, characters or their situations.

You can then go on to note more specific or detailed similarities. These may be to do with:

- the contexts in which the texts were written
- the settings or 'worlds' the texts present
- the writers' attitudes to the same subject or theme
- the narrative viewpoints they use
- how the texts are structured
- the tone of the writing, for instance serious, humorous, satirical, ironic or tragic
- the use of imagery or its absence
- vocabulary
- other stylistic features.

Then turn your attention to the **contrasts**. Concentrate on noting what makes the texts **different** in any of the above ways.

For example, look at a few of the ways we can connect and contrast two novels about the experiences of British visitors to India: E.M. Forster's *A Passage to India* and *Heat and Dust*, by Ruth Prawer Jhabvala.

Connections

- Both are set (at least partly) in India around 1923, when it was still part of the British Empire, but when the fight for Independence was beginning. They show India in transition. The resulting racial tension contributes to the plot and atmosphere of both novels.
- Both novels portray the world of the 'British Raj' – the expatriate community of officials who governed India at that time.
- Both have main characters who are English women new to the country and eager to experience 'the real India'. They find Anglo-India disturbing, cross boundaries of expected behaviour and become 'too involved' with Indians.
- The womens' concerns are disregarded by experienced Anglo-Indians – especially men – who put them down to the climate or old age.
- 'India always changes people,' says the narrator of *Heat and Dust*. This is illustrated in both novels.
- The 'heat and dust' of India are significant in both novels. They are part of the personality of India and are often used symbolically; rising temperatures and suffocating dust parallel and heighten the tension between individuals and races; the British struggle to keep the heat and dust (India) at bay, with barred windows and shutters.

Contrasts

- *A Passage to India* was written mainly in 1923–4, at the same time as the events it depicts. *Heat and Dust* was written in the 1970s, and with the benefit of hindsight it can present the transition in India in terms of the contrast between 'modern' India and India in the days of the Empire.

- Forster writes as an omniscient third-person narrator who sees into the minds of all his important characters, whether English or Indian, and moves freely from one perspective to another. *Heat and Dust* is a dual narrative. The story of Olivia, from 1923, is told in the third-person, but placed within a first-person frame or context. It is presented as if it has been researched and reconstructed from her letters by the main first-person narrator, her step-granddaughter, who intersperses it with entries from her diary of her own experience of travelling in India in the 1970s.

- Because of these narrative viewpoints, in *A Passage to India* Forster can describe English characters as they are seen by Indian characters as well as the other way round, while in *Heat and Dust*, Indians and Anglo-Indians are presented only as they are observed by English characters and not vice versa.

4 Formulate your question

So far, we have looked at a range of ways in which connections can be made between texts that share a theme. However, in your extended essay, you will not be required to write about all those aspects of the texts, but to choose one area to focus on in depth. From this, you will create your question. This needs careful thought, as a good question can make all the difference between a highly effective extended essay and a weak piece of writing with no clear direction. Your teacher should be able to help you to word your question in a way that will enable you to succeed.

The best questions:

- are well focused, on a limited, specific topic which you can explore in depth
- are challenging, but not too complex
- require you to analyse and compare the ways the writers have used language and literary techniques as well as themes; this is vital for achieving good grades.

Activity

If you have not already done so, devise your own extended essay question, making sure that you are clear about the key words and the ideas you intend to explore.

5 Research and note-taking

Now that you have a clear idea of your question, you will need to re-read the texts, but this time making careful notes, using annotations, highlighting, and any other methods you find helpful. Your aim is to find the material you require to make detailed comparisons. It is useful to have your own copies of texts for this task, so that you can make as many notes on them as you wish. In particular, look out for and highlight passages or scenes which are relevant to your theme, and which will provide you with examples and quotations to discuss. Passages that demonstrate clear parallels or contrasts between the texts will be especially useful.

Organizing you ideas

As you read and re-read your texts it may be useful to organize your ideas in a comparative format, such as using a table like the one below. If you are studying long prose texts you can use the table to contrast extracts based on similar themes. The more practice you get at thinking about texts in this way, the easier it will be to think comparatively about them in your exam.

	Extract 1	Extract 2
Subject		
Speaker/Situation		
Perspective/Tone		
Ideas/Message		
Atmosphere		
Imagery		
Language/ Vocabulary		
Context		

Activity

1 Find passages, scenes or poems from each of the texts you have chosen for your own extended essay, which offer you a clear opportunity to make detailed comparisons.

2 Make notes on how language and imagery are both used differently or similarly in each extract. Consider:

- your response to characters
- dialogue
- structure/form
- choice of vocabulary
- use of simile/metaphor
- the overall feeling, tone, or atmosphere that is generated.

3 Save your notes to help you when you write your extended essay.

Writing your essay

Now that you have become familiar with your texts, formulated your question, made notes and gathered your ideas, you are ready to begin the process of writing your extended essay.

The writing process involves several stages:

1 Planning

First, you need to structure your ideas and make a plan for your essay. Always keeping your question in mind, make a list of the main ideas and points you are going to explore and then arrange them in an order that will allow you to link them in a logical way.

2 The first draft

Very often, students find actually starting to write the essay quite difficult. In particular, it is common to get stuck when deciding on the starting point or the exact form of words of the first paragraph. The main thing at this stage, though, is to let go of the idea of perfection and get something down on paper that you can begin to develop. It is worth taking this approach to the essay as a whole, too. This is only the first draft of your essay and it is likely that quite extensive revision and editing will take place before you are happy with your final version. In fact, it would be extremely unusual – and not advisable – for a student to submit the first draft of an extended essay for assessment without any changes or revisions having been made.

Once you have completed the first draft, you can ask your teacher or supervisor to read it and give you some feedback. This will normally be in the form of general guidance. They will not be able to edit your essay in detail, but can point out which aspects of your work are successful and which need further development or improvement.

3 Revising and editing

Once you have done this you are ready to begin the task of revising and editing your work. Many students find at this point that they are trying to handle too much material, and need to use the revising and editing stage to select and organize their work more effectively. Be prepared to re-draft as much as you need to in order to produce a polished final piece of work.

All students have different ways of approaching revision and editing, but it can be useful to read through your work marking any alterations, deletions or amendments with a different coloured pen. Sections that require more extensive re-writing or alterations can be asterisked and numbered and new sections written and inserted.

If you are using a computer, it is possible to edit your work directly on-screen, but you will probably find it easier to work on a printed copy, which allows you to see all your work at once, rather than scrolling up and down. When your revisions are complete, you are ready to begin your final version.

4 The final version

Working from your revisions, you now need to write your final version. However, it is worth remembering when you are writing it that you can still make alterations to it even at this stage. If, in the course of your writing, you come across a section you are not happy with or a new idea strikes you that would improve your work further, then you can still make changes. The final version is only really 'final' when you have handed it in!

5 Presenting your essay

This is a major piece of coursework and it is important to present it in a way that will make a good impression. As well as being accurate, and typed or legibly written, it is good practice to acknowledge the sources you have used and any references you have made, directly or indirectly, to the words of someone else.

Obviously, in a literature essay, you will quote from the texts you are comparing. As long as you show those quotations clearly, using quotation marks, or for longer quotations, by indenting and separating them from the main body of your writing, you do not need to acknowledge them further.

If you have used information or critical writing from books other than the texts you are comparing, or from internet sources, you must acknowledge this clearly. Using material from sources without acknowledgement is known as plagiarism and is a form of malpractice that can have serious consequences. If plagiarism is discovered, the candidate concerned will not be awarded a qualification.

Sources are acknowledged using **references**, which can be presented in various ways.

- Number each reference as it crops up in your work. At the end of your essay make a numbered list of references, each linked to the corresponding number in the text. Each reference should give: the name of the author or editor of the book, the title of the book, the name of the publisher, the year it was published, and the page reference. It is rarely advisable to use references from the internet, but if you do, you need to include the whole web address, followed by the date on which you accessed the site.

- Alternatively, place the details of the reference in brackets in the main body of your essay, immediately after the quotation or reference.

Finally, add your **bibliography**. This should list all the books and other material that you have used in producing your essay. These should be in alphabetical order of the authors' surnames, and for each text, you should give details of: author(s)/ editor; title; date; place of publication; publisher.

Your teacher or supervisor will give you advice about how to do this if necessary (see the bibliography section in Chapter 4).

How your work will be assessed

Your teacher will make an initial assessment of your essay and then it will be passed on to an external moderator or examiner who will finalize your grade.

Four Assessment Objectives will be used to assess your work: AO1, AO2, AO3 and AO4. AO1 and AO2 are assessed together, and AO3 and AO4 are also assessed together.

AO1   Articulate creative, informed and relevant responses to literary texts, using appropriate terminology and concepts, and coherent, accurate written expression.

AO2   Demonstrate detailed critical understanding in analysing the ways in which structure, form and language shape meaning in literary texts.

AO3   Explore connections and comparisons between different literary texts, informed by interpretations of other readers.

AO4   Demonstrate understanding of the significance and influence of the contexts in which literary texts are written and received.

6 Revising for the examination

Objectives

- to plan revision for your exams
- to consider approaches to essay planning and working under timed conditions
- to prepare for comparative writing

Planning revision

The texts you have studied play a key role in your final assessment for either the AS or A Level course, and it is essential that you revise them very carefully in readiness for the exam. Your grade in these exams will depend on the quality and effectiveness of this preparation, so it is well worth planning how you intend to revise in good time. This is not a matter that you should put off until the last minute; hasty, inadequate revision could damage your chances of getting the grade you want. Students who do well show an independence of mind which reveals the ability to think for themselves, and to think clearly under the pressure of exam conditions. Revision is key to these skills.

Now let us have a look at some of the things that you can do to help revise your set texts and prepare yourself for the exam.

Reading, re-reading, and re-reading again

By this stage you will, no doubt, have read your texts a number of times. This reading and re-reading of the texts is essential to the development of your understanding and appreciation of them.

However, different kinds of reading are appropriate depending on why you are doing the reading. You may first read the text quickly, before you start to study it in detail. The next time you read it you will probably do so quite slowly in order to follow the plot carefully, to examine the ways in which the characters emerge, and to get used to the style of language used. Subsequent reads will be different again. You may skim through the text to quickly refresh your memory of the whole thing, or you may scan the text looking for particular references to images or ideas. These various readings are extremely important for a number of reasons:

- They help you to become very familiar with the text, not just in terms of the plot (although some books do need to be read several times just to understand what is happening), but also in terms of picking up on the details of the text. Most texts chosen for AS and A2 Level are very complex, and every time you read them you notice something new, something that you had not picked up the first, second, or even third time round.
- You tend to come to an understanding of a text over a period of time. You do not just read the text, understand it, and then find you are ready for the exam. The kinds of texts that you will have encountered in your AS and A2 Level studies need careful consideration. You need to allow yourself this thinking time in order to reflect on what you have read, to absorb the material, and then return to it again.

This kind of reading is part of a developmental process which enhances your knowledge and understanding of your set texts and therefore needs to be planned for over a period of time.

Time management

Time is a crucial factor in your revision programme. Building time into your programme for sufficient practice on a variety of tasks is vital. To do this, it is advisable to draw up a revision programme to cover the build-up to the final exams. This can be quite loose in the initial stages, but the closer you get to the exams, the tighter it needs to be. Make sure that you cover every aspect of the assessment. Here are some points to consider when devising your revision programme:

- Be realistic – do not overestimate how much you can get through in a given time. It is far better to start your revision programme earlier than to try to cram everything in at the last minute.

- Make sure that your programme gives the necessary attention to every text. Do not rely on the 'I know that text well enough so I don't need to revise it' approach. Often, when you come to revise a text that you studied months before, you remember things about it that you had forgotten or that had become hazy.

- Aim for variety in your revision tasks. Create a balance between revision activities which are reading-based and those which involve writing tasks. For example, as well as the various reading activities, there are those involving written responses, such as practice on specimen papers, timed essays or essay planning, which are described in the rest of this chapter. If possible, you should also watch videos related to your texts, or listen to recordings of them.

- Build in to your programme some time off to relax. You will not work at your best if you spend all your time studying. Revision is best done with a fresh mind and in relatively short sessions with breaks. You can only take in so much at one sitting. One to two hours at a stretch is enough.

It is important to keep a good balance between texts. Even if you feel you know a text really well, do not skimp on the revision of it. Remember, though, that a revision programme will need to be flexible in order to cater for the unexpected. Allow yourself time to think about questions and ideas. Also, beware of wasting too much valuable revision time trying to create the perfect programme.

Activity

Try planning out a short revision programme for yourself lasting a week, taking account of all the points mentioned above.

Past-paper and specimen paper questions

As part of your revision programme, try to look at as many questions from past or specimen papers as you can. The value of this lies in giving you the flavour of the question types that Chief Examiners set. Certainly, looking at past-paper questions on your texts will show you a range of topics that questions have focused on in the past, and sometimes similar questions do appear again. However, do not learn model answers and hope to be able to use these in the exam. If you come across specimen or model answers, regard them critically and as one possible way of answering, but do not take them to be the definitive answer. Remember, in the exam you will be expected to respond using your own ideas and thoughts, and examiners can tell immediately if you are parroting a model answer you have learned.

> ### Activity
> Gather as many questions as you can on the texts that you have studied. Draft out a rough essay plan for each of these questions. (Do not spend more than two or three minutes on each plan.)

As well as giving you ideas of the types of things that have been asked about before, looking at past-paper questions will also give you a clear idea of how questions can be worded and the style in which they are presented. The more you know in this respect, the less likely you are to be thrown by question phrasing or terminology. Looking at past papers can also expose gaps in your knowledge of a set text and allow you to remedy this.

Timed essays

One of the main worries that students have in terms of answering on their set texts is how they are going to get all their ideas down in the time allowed. For this reason it is extremely important that you get a good deal of practice writing under timed conditions. You will, no doubt, do some timed pieces in class, but there is no reason why you should not practise them at home as well. All you need are some suitable questions, a quiet place and some time. In one sense it does not even matter if the work is not marked (although obviously you will get even more benefit from it if it is) – what really matters is building up your experience of writing against the clock. One thing is certain – the more you practice, the quicker you will get. It really will help you to speed up and it will also show you how much information you can deal with in a specified time and how well you can plan under timed conditions.

Essay planning

Practice in essay planning should form another key part in your revision process. The best essays are those where students have thought about what they want to say before they actually start to write. By planning essays you can ensure that your argument is coherent and that you are using your knowledge and evidence to best effect. Essays that are not planned can easily drift away from the main point of the question or become rambling and jumbled.

In the exam itself you will have little time to spend on planning; you will feel an in-built pressure to start writing as soon as possible. However, what you do in that first two or three minutes after reading the question can be vital to the success of your answer. Practice in the build-up to the exam will help you to develop the skills to plan quickly and effectively. There are a number of things you can do to help.

- Read the question very carefully and make sure that you understand all parts of it.
- Analyse the question and note down the key topic areas it deals with.
- Briefly plan how you intend to deal with these areas – this may mean only three or four points each summed up in a few words. The main thing is that you will have a checklist of the points you are going to cover before you begin writing your essay.

Immediately after reading the question, it is likely that ideas will run through your mind very quickly. If you do not get these down on paper in the form of a rough plan, there is a chance you might miss out an important point in the finished essay.

As well as doing your timed essays it will also be useful preparation if you can do essay plans for as many questions as you can. This will help to get you into the routine of planning but it will also give you the opportunity to think about a wide variety of issues related to your set texts.

There are many ways in which you can create your essay plans. Some students prefer to create a 'spidergram' or 'pattern notes', while others prefer a linear or flow-diagram approach. Many students find a straightforward list of points the most helpful. You will need to find the method that suits your way of thinking best and which allows you to plan your work most effectively.

Writing your essay

Having completed your plan, you are ready to write your essay. Here are some things to bear in mind:

- Always begin your essay by addressing the question directly. It can be a very useful technique to actually use some of the words of the question in your introduction. Your introduction should give a general indication of your response to the question or summarize the approach you intend to take, perhaps stating your viewpoint. The introduction might consist of your basic essay plan, expanded a little. However, keep the introduction brief and never include biographical information or plot summary.

- An alternative way to begin your essay, and one that can be very effective, is to respond to the question by starting with a strong, perhaps contentious idea that captures the reader's attention immediately. This will launch you straight into points that will support your argument.

- Develop your points clearly using evidence and references to the text to support your ideas.

- Assume that the examiner has read the text you are writing about and knows it extremely well, so there is no need to explain the plot or who the characters are.

- Make sure that your essay deals with all parts of the question.

- If your answer is similar to an essay you have written before, make sure that you are being relevant at all times and are not simply regurgitating a set answer that is in your mind. Also, avoid rehashing your notes as an answer to a question.

- Where you use quotations, make sure that they are short and relevant. Do not copy out chunks of the text.

- Make sure that your essay has a conclusion in which you sum up your arguments and analysis. It is often through the conclusion that the relevance of certain points you have made is brought into focus and the essay is given a sense of unity and completeness.

Throughout your revision period, bear in mind what you will be expected to show in the exam. Some factual knowledge will be required, but not much. That you know the facts about a text, the story-line and who the characters are, will be taken as read. The emphasis will be on showing judgement, analysis, sensitivity and perception in your responses.

7 The Examiner's view

Objectives

- to think about the things examiners and moderators look for in the work they mark
- to understand how your work will be assessed

What the Examiner looks for

An important person in the process of your assessment at AS or A2 Level is the Examiner who will mark or moderate your work. Examiners are not some special breed of people who spend their lives marking exam scripts. For the most part, they are practising teachers who work with students like yourself helping them to prepare for exams. However, they can only mark the work that you present them with, and the mark that is awarded depends *solely* on its quality.

It is a fallacy that one Examiner might be more generous with you than another. Careful procedures are followed to ensure that the mark you receive from one Examiner is just the same as the mark you would receive if another assessed your work. Indeed, it is not simply a case of one Examiner looking at your work and giving a mark. Exam scripts go through a number of processes which involve responses being looked at by several people before a final mark is awarded. How well you do is up to you, not the Examiner.

It is also worth dispelling another misconception that some students have concerning the role of the Examiner. They picture the Examiner as some kind of merciless inquisitor who takes delight in catching them out. Examiners, so the thinking goes, look only for negative aspects in responses and ruthlessly dismantle every essay that they come across. Questions are their tools, designed to catch students out.

In fact, nothing could be further from the truth. Questions are designed to let you show your knowledge to the best of your ability. Obviously Examiners will not reward qualities which are not present in your responses, but they will look for the positive features in your work. Examiners take far more pleasure and satisfaction in reading good quality material that they can reward than they do in poor work that must be awarded poor marks. Think of the Examiner as an interested audience for your writing, who will award marks fairly and look favourably on responses wherever there are positive qualities to be found.

Bearing in mind the large number of students who sit exams in AS and A2 Level Literature each year, it is very encouraging that Examiners report that few candidates reveal lack of knowledge, skills, or preparation, and very weak answers are extremely uncommon. The vast majority of students show that they have prepared themselves to the best of their abilities for the papers. However, there are aspects of the exam that Examiners often comment on as areas that need more careful preparation. We will now go on to consider some of these.

The questions

The questions that you will be asked will not be prescriptive. They will be open questions that will invite you to debate the issues or express an opinion on a particular view, and encourage you to develop informed judgements on the texts and the issues they raise. It is these judgements that the Examiner is interested in reading about.

Where the question contains some kind of proposition, you are never expected to simply accept it. Acceptance or rejection needs to be supported with evidence and justification. One criticism frequently made by Examiners is that a student simply agrees with or rejects the proposition and then goes on to write about something else entirely. This still happens with worrying regularity. The key is to read the question and do what it says.

Set texts

You will study a number of set texts for this specification.

- In Unit 1 you will study the work of one of four prescribed poets. You will also choose one novel from a list of set texts.
- In Unit 3 you will choose one of four Shakespeare plays for study. You will also choose one drama text and one poetry text from a prescribed list.

In addition you will also study a number of other texts throughout the course as part of your wider reading or coursework.

Technical accuracy

The ideas that you express in your answers or your coursework are of primary importance. However, these ideas will be not presented most effectively if your writing suffers from various technical inaccuracies. It is, therefore, crucial that your answers are as free from technical errors as you can make them.

There are several points that examiners draw attention to in this respect.

- **Punctuation:** Ensure that you use full stops, commas, quotation marks, and so on, where appropriate. It is easy for these things to be forgotten in the heat of the exam, but poor punctuation can mean that your ideas are communicated to the reader less effectively and this may affect your mark.
- **Sentences:** Make sure that you write in complete sentences and that you avoid long, convoluted ones.
- **Paragraphing:** Few candidates fail to use paragraphs at all, but examiners often point to the inappropriate use of paragraphs. For example, one-sentence paragraphs should be avoided and so should excessively long paragraphs.
- **Vocabulary:** Try to vary your vocabulary without becoming verbose simply to make your essay sound more 'impressive'.
- **Spelling:** Obviously you should try to make your work free of spelling errors. However, when writing under exam conditions some errors may well creep in. You should do your best to check each answer as you complete it to keep these to a minimum. If nothing else, though, make sure that you are spelling the titles of the texts, the names of the characters, and the names of the authors correctly. It does not give a good impression if, after two years' study, you are still writing about 'Shakespear's play' or 'Jayne Austin's novel'.

- **Cliché, flattery, and slang:** Avoid the use of well-worn phrases such as 'Jane Eyre is a victim of male domination' or 'Lear acts like a man possessed'. Flattery towards authors, such as 'Shakespeare's portrayal of a man in emotional turmoil is second to none' or 'It is clear that Hardy is one of the giants of English poetry' are equally to be avoided. Also avoid slang expressions, such as 'Oskar Schindler is a bit of a Del-boy character' or 'Laertes goes ballistic when he hears about his father's death'.

- **Quotation:** If you are using quotation, make sure it is accurate. If you have the book with you in the exam there is really no excuse for misquoting (although it still happens). If you are relying on memory, it is very easy to misquote. Perhaps all that needs to be said is that it is better not to use a quotation than to misquote, or worse still 'invent' a quote based on a rough idea of how it goes.

Model and prepared answers

Examiners report that they do not see model or prepared answers anywhere near as frequently as they used to in student responses. However, they do still crop up from time to time. There is nothing wrong with reading model answers during the course of your study, as long as you use them wisely. They can be useful in suggesting new ideas, but be aware that they present just one way of answering a question. The Examiner is interested in what *you* have to say on a particular topic or question, not what the writer of a prepared answer has to say.

Remember that the best responses are those in which your own voice can be heard. The whole point of the course that you are studying is to develop your ability to write confidently, relevantly, and thoughtfully about your ideas on the texts you have studied. Do not be afraid to use the pronoun 'I' occasionally in your essays and do not be afraid to respond genuinely to a question. Attempts to memorize prepared answers never work.

How the Examiner will mark your work

Above all, Examiners marking AS or A2 Level English Literature scripts are trained to be positive and flexible. The Examiners (each of your exam papers is usually marked by a separate Examiner) will look for the positive qualities in your work. They will not approach your response with a preconceived idea of an 'ideal answer' but will have an open mind. They will evaluate your efforts to provide an informed personal response to the question.

Answering the question

Examiners are always aware of students who do not read the questions carefully enough. You should make absolutely sure that you are well trained in studying carefully the exact wording of the question or task. Remember that the question or task set should be the whole basis and framework of your response. The views, opinions and ideas you explore are up to you (providing you can support them through close reference and analysis of the text, and they fulfil the demands of the task you have been set).

Length

In written exam answers, Examiners do not award marks on the basis of the length of your essay but they will look for what you have achieved in your writing. An essay can appear brief but on closer inspection it may be a succinct and well-argued response and therefore worthy of a high mark. It is true to say, though, that essays that are very short often lack sufficient depth in the development of ideas. On the other hand, over-long essays can become repetitive, rambling and lacking in a coherent structure. Do your best to create a balanced answer.

Descriptors

In addition to the question-specific guidance that Examiners are given, exam boards also provide them with 'descriptors' to help them to place your essay in a particular mark band. These describe the typical features of responses at different levels, and are linked to the Assessment Objectives being tested.

In reading the descriptors you will see the key features that can bring you success in the exam, and to achieve them there are some basic things you can do. In fact if you are to achieve success there are certain things that you *must* do. You must make sure that:

- you have read your texts carefully several times
- you know your texts thoroughly
- you are fully aware of the issues, ideas and themes they contain
- you are aware of the stylistic features of the texts you have studied
- you can support your ideas and comments effectively.

Remember: The secret of success is to be well prepared. Know your material and know what you think about it. Be aware of the Assessment Objectives that you are being tested on and make sure that you address these objectives.

List of terms

Allegory: an allegory is a story or narrative, often told at some length, which has a deeper meaning below the surface. *The Pilgrim's Progress* by John Bunyan is a well-known allegory. A more modern example is George Orwell's *Animal Farm*, which on a surface level is about a group of animals who take over their farm but on a deeper level is an allegory of the Russian Revolution and the shortcomings of Communism.

Alliteration: the repetition of the same consonant sound, especially at the beginnings of words. For example: 'Five miles meandering with a mazy motion' (*Kubla Khan* by S.T. Coleridge).

Allusion: a reference to another event, person, place, or work of literature – the allusion is usually implied rather than explicit and often provides another layer of meaning to what is being said.

Ambiguity: use of language where the meaning is unclear or has two or more possible interpretations or meanings. It could be created through a weakness in the way the writer has expressed himself or herself but often it is used by writers quite deliberately to create layers of meaning in the mind of the reader.

Ambivalence: this indicates more than one possible attitude is being displayed by the writer towards a character, theme or idea.

Anachronism: something that is historically inaccurate, for example the reference to a clock chiming in Shakespeare's *Julius Caesar*.

Anthropomorphism: the endowment of something that is not human with human characteristics.

Antithesis: contrasting ideas or words that are balanced against each other.

Apostrophe: an interruption in a poem or narrative so that the speaker or writer can address a dead or absent person or particular audience directly.

Archaic: language that is old-fashioned. It may not be completely obsolete but it will no longer be in currect use.

Assonance: the repetition of similar vowel sounds. For example: 'There must be Gods thrown down and trumpets blown' (*Hyperion* by John Keats). This shows the paired assonance of 'must', 'trum-', 'thrown', 'blown'.

Atmosphere: the prevailing mood created by a piece of writing.

Ballad: a narrative poem that tells a story (traditional ballads were songs), usually in a straightforward way. The theme is often tragic or contains a whimsical, supernatural or fantastical element.

Bathos: an anti-climax or sudden descent from the serious to the ridiculous – sometimes deliberate, sometimes unintentional, on the part of the writer.

Blank verse: unrhymed poetry that adheres to a strict pattern in that each line is an iambic pentameter (a ten-syllable line with five stresses). It is close to the rhythm of speech or prose and is used a great deal by many writers including Shakespeare and Milton.

Caesura: a conscious break in a line of poetry.

Caricature: a character often described through the exaggeration of a small number of features that he or she possesses.

Catharsis: a purging of the emotions which takes place at the end of a tragedy.

Cliché: a phrase, idea or image that has been used so much that is has lost much of its original meaning, impact and freshness.

Colloquial: ordinary, everyday speech and language.

Comedy: originally simply a play or other work which ended happily. Now we use this term to describe something that is funny and which makes us laugh. In literature the comedy is not necessarily a lightweight form. A play like *Measure for Measure* by William Shakespeare for example, is for the most part a serious and dark play, but as it ends happily, it is described as a comedy.

Conceit: an elaborate, extended, and sometimes surprising comparison between things that, at first sight, do not have much in common.

Connotation: an implication or association attached to a word or phrase. A connotation is suggested or felt rather than being explicit.

Consonance: the repetition of the same consonant sounds in two or more words in which the vowel sounds are different. For example: 'And by his smile, I knew that sullen hall,/ By his dead smile I knew we stood in Hell' (*Strange Meeting* by Wilfred Owen). Where consonance replaces the rhyme, as here, it is called half-rhyme.

Couplet: two consecutive lines of verse that rhyme.

Dénouement: the ending of a play, novel, or drama where 'all is revealed' and the plot is made clear.

Diction: the choice of words that a writer makes. Another term for vocabulary.

Didactic: intending to preach or teach; didactic works often contain a particular moral or political point.

Dramatic monologue: a poem or prose piece in which a character addresses an audience. Often the monologue is complete in itself, as in Alan Bennett's *Talking Heads*.

Elegy: a meditative poem, usually sad and reflective in nature. Sometimes, though not always, it is concerned with the theme of death.

Empathy: a feeling on the part of the reader of sharing the particular experience being described by the character or writer.

End stopping: ending a verse line with a pause or a stop.

Enjambement: where a line of verse flows on into the next line without a pause.

Epic: a long narrative poem, written in an elevated style and usually dealing with a heroic theme or story. Homer's *The Iliad* and Milton's *Paradise Lost* are examples of this.

Euphemism: the expression of an unpleasant or unsavoury idea in a less blunt and more pleasant way.

Euphony: use of pleasant or melodious sounds.

Exemplum: a story that contains or illustrates a moral point, put forward as an 'example'.

Fable: a short story that presents a clear moral lesson.

Fabliau: a short comic tale with a bawdy element, akin to the 'dirty story'. Chaucer's *The Miller's Tale* contains strong elements of the fabliau.

Farce: a play that aims to entertain the audience through absurd and ridiculous characters and actions.

Feminine ending: an extra unstressed syllable at the end of a line of poetry. (Contrast with a stressed syllable, a masculine ending.)

Figurative language: language that is symbolic or metaphorical and not meant to be taken literally.

Foot: a group of syllables forming a unit of verse – the basic unit of 'metre'.

Free verse: verse written without any fixed structure (either in metre or rhyme).

Genre: a particular type of writing, for instance prose, poetry, drama.

Heptameter: a verse line containing seven feet.

Hexameter: a verse line containing six feet.

Hyperbole: deliberate and extravagant exaggeration.

Iamb: the most common metrical foot in English poetry, consisting of an unstressed syllable followed by a stressed syllable.

Idyll: a story, often written in verse, usually concerning innocent and rustic characters in rural, idealized surroundings. This form can also deal with more heroic subjects, as in Tennyson's *Idylls of the King*. (See **Pastoral**.)

Imagery: the use of words to create a picture or image in the mind of the reader. Images can relate to any of the senses, not just sight, but also hearing, taste, touch and smell. It often refers to the use of descriptive language, particularly metaphors and similes.

Internal rhyme: rhyming words within a line rather than at the end of lines.

Inter-textual: having clear links with other texts through the themes, ideas or issues which are explored.

Irony: at its simplest level, irony means saying one thing while meaning another. It occurs where a word or phrase has one surface meaning but another contradictory, possibly opposite meaning is implied. Irony is frequently confused with sarcasm. Sarcasm is spoken, often relying on tone of voice and is much more blunt than irony.

Lament: a poem expressing intense grief.

Lyric: originally a song performed to the accompaniment of a lyre (an early harp-like instrument), but now it can mean a song-like poem or a short poem expressing personal feeling.

Metaphor: a comparison of one thing to another in order to make description more vivid. The metaphor actually states that one thing *is* the other. For example, the simile would be: 'The huge knight stood like an impregnable tower in the ranks of the enemy', whereas the metaphor would be: 'The huge knight was an impregnable tower in the ranks of the enemy'. (See **Simile** and **Personification**.)

Metre: the regular use of stressed and unstressed syllables in poetry.

Mock heroic: a poem that treats trivial subject matter in the grand and elevated style of epic poetry. The effect produced is often humerous, as in Pope's *The Rape of the Lock*.

Monometer: a verse line consisting of only one metrical foot.

Motif: a dominant theme, subject or idea which runs through a piece of literature. Often a 'motif' can assume a symbolic importance.

Narrative: a piece of writing that tells a story.

Octameter: a verse line consisting of eight feet.

Octave: the first eight lines of a sonnet.

Ode: a verse form similar to a lyric but often more lengthy and containing more serious and elevated thoughts.

Onomatopoeia: the use of words whose sound reflects the sound of the thing or process that they describe. On a simple level, words like 'bang', 'hiss' and 'splash' are onomatopoeic, but the device also has more subtle uses.

Oxymoron: a figure of speech which joins together words of opposite meanings, for instance 'the living dead', 'bitter sweet', and so on.

Paradox: a statement that appears contradictory, but when considered more closely is seen to contain a good deal of truth.

Parody: a work that is written in imitation of another work, very often with the intention of making fun of the original.

Pastoral: generally literature concerning rural life with idealized settings and rustic characters. Often pastorals are concerned with the lives of shepherds and shepherdesses presented in idyllic and unrealistic ways. (See **Idyll**.)

Pathos: the effect in literature which makes the reader feel sadness or pity.

Pentameter: a line of verse containing five feet.

Periphrasis: an indirect, roundabout or long-winded way of expressing something.

Personification: the attribution of human feelings, emotions or sensations to an inanimate object. Personification is a kind of metaphor where human qualities are given to things or abstract ideas.

Plot: the sequence of events in a poem, play, novel or short story that make up the main storyline.

Prose: any kind of writing which is not verse – usually divided into fiction and non-fiction.

Protagonist: the main character or speaker in a poem, monologue, play or story.

Pun: a play on words that have similar sounds but quite different meanings.

Quatrain: a stanza of four lines, which can have various rhyme schemes.

Refrain: repetition throughout a poem of a phrase, line or series of lines, as in the 'chorus' of a song.

Rhetoric: originally the art of speaking and writing in such a way as to persuade an audience to a particular point of view. Now it is often used to imply grand words that have no substance to them. There are a variety of rhetorical devices such as the rhetorical question – a question which does not require an answer as the answer is either obvious or implied in the question itself. (See **Apostrophe**, **Exemplum**.)

Rhyme: corresponding sounds in words, usually at the end of each line but not always. (See **Internal Rhyme**.)

Rhyme scheme: the pattern of the rhymes in a poem.

Rhythm: the 'movement' of the poem as created through the metre and the way that language is stressed within the poem.

Satire: the highlighting or exposing of human failings or foolishness within a society through ridiculing them. Satire can range from being gentle and light to being extremely biting and bitter in tone, for instance Swift's *Gulliver's Travels* or *A Modest Proposal* and George Orwell's *Animal Farm*.

Scansion: the analysis of metrical patterns in poetry.

Septet: a seven-line stanza.

Sestet: the last six lines of a sonnet.

Simile: a comparison of one thing to another in order to make description more vivid. Similes use the words 'like' or 'as' in this comparison. (See **Metaphor**.)

Soliloquy: a speech in which a character, alone on stage, expresses his or her thoughts and feelings aloud for the benefit of the audience.

Sonnet: a fourteen-line poem, usually with ten syllables in each line. There are several ways in which the lines can be organized, but often they consist of an octave and a sestet.

Stanza: the blocks of lines into which a poem is divided. (Sometimes these are, less precisely, referred to as verses, which can lead to confusion as poetry is sometimes called 'verse'.)

Stream of consciousness: a technique by which the writer reveals their thoughts and emotions in a 'stream' as they come to mind, without giving order or structure.

Structure: the way that a poem or play or other piece of writing has been put together. This can include the metre pattern, stanza arrangement and the way the ideas are developed, etc.

Style: the individual way in which a writer has used language to express his or her ideas.

Sub-plot: a secondary storyline in a story or play. Often, as in some Shakespeare plays, the sub-plot can provide some comic relief from the main action, but sub-plots can also relate in quite complex ways to the main plot of a text.

Sub-text: ideas, themes, or issues that are not dealt with overtly by a text but which exist below the surface meaning of it.

Symbol: like images, symbols represent something else. In very simple terms a red rose is often used to symbolize love; distant thunder is often symbolic of approaching trouble. Symbols can be very subtle and multi-layered in their significance.

Syntax: the way in which sentences are structured. Sentences can be structured in different ways to achieve different effects.

Tetrameter: a verse line of four feet.

Theme: the central idea or ideas that the writer explores through a text.

Tone: the tone of a text is created through the combined effects of a number of features, such as diction, syntax and rhythm. The tone is a major factor in establishing the overall impression of the piece of writing.

Trimeter: a verse line consisting of three feet.

Zeugma: a device that joins together two apparently incongruous things by applying a verb or adjective to them which only really applies to one of them, for example: 'Kill the boys and the luggage' (Shakespeare's *Henry V*).